Panic Stations

A Farce

Derek Benfield

Samuel French - London

PANIC STATIONS

CHARACTERS

(in order of appearance)

ABEL BOUNTY

CHESTER DREADNOUGHT

CAROL

PATRICIA

LADY ELROOD

MISS PARTRIDGE

LORD ELROOD

SERGEANT EVEREST

MRS BOUNTY

It all happens in an old country cottage in the Spring.

ACT   I   Afternoon

ACT II

    Scene 1   Early evening

    Scene 2   Half an hour later

"PANIC STATIONS"
GROUND PLAN

EXTERIOR BACKING

INTERIOR BACKING

DOOR

FIRE BACKING

FIREPLACE

ROSTRUM

STEPS

WINDOW

FRONT DOOR

SOFA

TABLE

COFFEE TABLE

SMALL CHAIR

SEAT

WINDOW

DOOR

INTERIOR BACKING

PANIC STATIONS

ACT ONE

An old but attractive cottage in the country. Through the windows you can see (on a clear day) fields and a pond. Oak beams and that sort of thing. A staircase U.L.C. leading up and off to the L. A heavy front door U.R.C. A large open hearth L. where a log fire sometimes burns. A door D.L. leads to the kitchen, and another door D.R. to the cellar. There are two windows: one U.C. and one R. between the two doors, with a padded window seat. A large sofa is set L. at a slight angle towards the fireplace, with a small table R. of it and a low coffee table in front of it. A small tub chair could be R.C. but it is not essential if space is limited. The place has obviously been empty for some time. A few cobwebs here and there. The windows dirty. A general untidiness and feeling of damp.

It is raining outside. Pouring down. So, though it is the middle of the afternoon, a lamp is alight.

Someone is knocking at the door. Whoever it is is getting impatient, which is not surprising as they must be soaked waiting out there. After a while a man appears at the top of the stairs. He is middle-aged and grubby, a local odd-job man. His name is ABEL BOUNTY. He makes unhurriedly for the door, muttering the while.

ABEL   All right! All right!   I'm coming! All right!
                All right –

                (The visitor knocks again.)

                Knock! Knock! Knock! I'm coming. All right. All
                right –

(He arrives in his own good time and opens the front
door. The wind and the rain meet him and push the
door open so that ABEL is hidden behind it. A wet
young man with two suitcases bursts in. He is
wearing a soaking raincoat and a hat. His name is
CHESTER DREADNOUGHT, and he moves to C.

He looks back at the open door but cannot see ABEL
behind it. He looks puzzled, turns away to put down
the cases and takes off his hat. ABEL shuts the
door with a bang. CHESTER jumps with fright,
turns and sees him.

CHESTER	Well? Where were you?
ABEL	Behind the door.
CHESTER	Not then! Before!
	(ABEL comes down to CHESTER.)
ABEL	Before what?
CHESTER	When I was out and you were in.
ABEL	I was upstairs. Seeing to meself.
CHESTER	Well, I wish you'd see to yourself another time. I was out there and wet.
ABEL	I can see that.
CHESTER	And I've never known such wet in all my life.
ABEL	You wait till the winter.
CHESTER	(alarmed) You mean the winter wet's worse?
ABEL	Makes this look like an April shower.
CHESTER	Good God! (He takes off his coat, flaps off the rain and puts it down on the banisters.)
ABEL	You staying, then?
CHESTER	Well, I'm not going out there again!
ABEL	(realising) Ah - P'raps you're the one who's coming here?
CHESTER	Yes. I am and I have.
ABEL	That's all right, then.

CHESTER   I don't know about that. (Moves D. L. of the sofa,
                    looking about.)   It looked better in the sunshine.

                    (ABEL starts looking for something in his pockets.)

ABEL   I've got your name written down somewhere.

CHESTER   It doesn't matter.

ABEL   I'll find it in a minute.

CHESTER   You don't have to bother.

ABEL   Can't remember it without my bit of paper, can I?

CHESTER   No, but I can. Chester Dreadnought.

ABEL   That's right!

CHESTER   That's me.

ABEL   (moving R. of sofa)   So you must be what I'm
                    expecting.

CHESTER   And are you what I'm expecting?

ABEL   I dunno what that is, do I?

CHESTER   A man to help me move in and get ready.

ABEL   That's right! I'm Abel.   (He crosses to CHESTER.)

CHESTER   Yes, I'm sure you are, but -

ABEL   Abel Bounty.

CHESTER   Oh, that's your name?

ABEL   That's right.

CHESTER   Well, Mr Bounty, we'll soon get this place shipshape
                    between us.   (Seeing some cobwebs on the fire-
                    place.)   Ah-ha! You missed some here.

ABEL   I had my wife over this morning.

CHESTER   Did you?

ABEL   She said she'd give me a hand with the cleaning.

CHESTER   Well, you didn't get very far down here.   (He
                    crosses to D. R. C. and picks up some paper from
                    the floor.)

ABEL   We started upstairs in the bedroom and carried on

	all morning.
CHESTER	You were supposed to be doing the cleaning.
ABEL	We got farther up there than we did down here.
CHESTER	Yes, I'm sure you did!
ABEL	Tidied up the rooms and made the beds.
CHESTER	Oh, I see.
ABEL	(moving to L. of CHESTER) So now we can finish off down here.
CHESTER	Finish off? You haven't started.
ABEL	Won't take long with three of us.
CHESTER	Oh, your wife's still here, then?
ABEL	No, no. She had to go home.
CHESTER	But I thought you said –
ABEL	Three pairs of hands will do this in no time.

(CHESTER looks puzzled, makes sure he has only two hands, glances at ABEL to check also. Can't understand it.)

CHESTER	Three pairs?
ABEL	Two down here and one up there.
CHESTER	One up there?
ABEL	(with a grin) That is, if she's come here to work!

(CHESTER considers this.)

CHESTER	Who?
ABEL	The one upstairs. (He chuckles to himself.) She's got a pair all right.
CHESTER	I beg your pardon?
ABEL	I couldn't help but notice, could I?
CHESTER	Couldn't you?
ABEL	Well, I mean to say –
CHESTER	What?

ABEL   Well, mine went out and yours came in.

CHESTER   Let's get this straight. Your wife carried on all
              morning and then went home?

ABEL   That's right.

CHESTER   Leaving you here alone?

ABEL   Yes.

CHESTER   Then I arrived and that made two.

ABEL   Two down here and one up there.

CHESTER   But the one up there went home!

ABEL   That was mine. And mine went out and yours came
              in.

CHESTER   But mine hasn't got here yet!

ABEL   I wouldn't be too sure about that.

CHESTER   She's coming on later. I said I'd go on ahead and
              get everything ready. I didn't want her to see down
              here like this.   (He crosses to below the sofa.)

ABEL   And now you won't want her to see upstairs like
              that!   (He chuckles.)

CHESTER   What do you mean?

ABEL   Well - if mine's been and gone, and yours hasn't
              come, whose is up there?

CHESTER   (hopefully)   Your sister?

ABEL   My sister hasn't got a pair like that!

              (CHESTER goes to L. of table.)

CHESTER   Look, Mr Bounty, this pair of hands -

ABEL   The upstairs pair?

CHESTER   Yes. Do they belong to a - ?

ABEL   Oh, yes!

CHESTER   That's what I thought. Is she - er - ?

ABEL   Oh, yes!

CHESTER   She would be. Well, what's she doing here?

ABEL   She went upstairs to take her clothes off.

CHESTER   You mean to say a perfectly strange girl arrived on the doorstep and said, 'I've come to take my clothes off'?

ABEL   Well - she was all wet, you see. Same as you.

CHESTER   I haven't taken my clothes off.

ABEL   You had your coat on, though, hadn't you? You didn't arrive in a dress.

CHESTER   Well, I thought a coat would be better.

ABEL   So there you are, sir. That's how it was and what it is.

CHESTER   Well, what it is isn't what it should be, so you'd better be quick and make it what it was.

ABEL   What it was when?

CHESTER   Before this other pair of hands arrived.

ABEL   I can't do that.

CHESTER   Why not?

ABEL   Turn her out in the rain with no clothes on?

CHESTER   She can borrow my coat. I can't think why you let in a strange pair of hands in a wet dress in the first place.

                (The strange pair of hands appears at the top of the stairs. She is in her twenties, very pretty, and is wearing a cute dressing-gown that is collaborating with her figure. Her name is CAROL.)

CAROL   Hullo -

                (CHESTER turns and sees her.)

CHESTER   Oh, my God!

ABEL   See what I mean, sir?

CHESTER   Yes, I do. Very much.

ABEL   You can imagine her standing at the door in a wet dress, can't you?

CHESTER   (smiling enthusiastically)   Yes, I certainly can!
                (He quickly collects himself and becomes stern.)

	I mean, yes, I can.
ABEL	Well, I mean to say -
CHESTER	Abel, I ordered some drink. Did it arrive?
ABEL	(with relish) Oh, yes. Arrived yesterday, that did.
CHESTER	Well, I hope there's some left for me.
ABEL	I'll go and see, sir. (He goes towards the kitchen.)

(CAROL comes down the stairs to CHESTER. He is trying not to notice her obvious attractions. ABEL pauses at the kitchen door.)

	See what I mean, sir?
CHESTER	What?
ABEL	I could hardly turn away a pair of hands like that, could I? (He goes, chuckling to himself.)
CAROL	Isn't he sweet?
CHESTER	I suppose I shall get used to him in time. (He indicates the state of the room.) It's not very tidy, I'm afraid.
CAROL	We'll soon see to it.
CHESTER	Will we?
CAROL	That's one of the things I'm here for.
CHESTER	Wh - what are the others?
CAROL	I expect we'll think of something.
CHESTER	I say - you must be awfully cold like that.
CAROL	That's very kind of you.
CHESTER	What?

(She has assumed he is offering to keep her warm and closes to him, putting her head on his chest and holding him around the waist. He is uncertain what to do with his arms. Eventually leaves them hanging limply at his sides.)

I say, look - er - Well, I - H'm. Oh, dear.
(A pause.)   You can borrow my coat if you like.

CAROL	It's all wet.
CHESTER	So it is.
CAROL	This is much nicer.
	(She pushes his elbows smartly upwards so that his arms are suddenly around the back of her neck. She snuggles into him. ABEL returns.)
ABEL	You two seem to be getting to know each other.
	(CHESTER breaks away quickly. ABEL has brought with him two glasses and a bottle of whisky, two-thirds full,which he puts on the table R. of the sofa.)
	There you are, sir.
	(CHESTER goes to look at the bottle and reacts to the level.)
CHESTER	Is this how it arrived?
ABEL	(plausibly) Oh, yes.
CHESTER	But it's not full.
ABEL	That's what it was and how it is, sir.
CHESTER	Abel –
ABEL	Well – I did have a small sip. On account of the damp. I knew you wouldn't mind. Just a thimbleful.
CHESTER	Looks more like a bucketful!
ABEL	(going) I'll leave you to it, then.
CHESTER	What?
ABEL	I've a bit more to do in the kitchen, so I'll carry on out there while you carry on in here. (He goes.)
	(CHESTER pours two whiskies.)
CHESTER	Whisky?
CAROL	What?
CHESTER	It'll warm you up.
CAROL	I was warming up.
CHESTER	Yes – but I think you'd better do it with whisky. (Gives her a drink.) Cheers.

CAROL	Cheers.
	(They drink.)
	You seemed awfully surprised to see me.
CHESTER	Did I?
CAROL	You jumped.
CHESTER	Yes. I often do that. I often jump when I'm surprised. I go, 'Oh!' (He jumps.) Silly, isn't it?
CAROL	Almost as if you weren't expecting me.
CHESTER	Really?
CAROL	If I hadn't known better I'd have thought that was what it was.
CHESTER	Yes.
CAROL	What do you mean, 'Yes'?
CHESTER	I mean that's what it was and how it is. I wasn't.
CAROL	Wasn't what?
CHESTER	Expecting you.
CAROL	Don't tell me you've forgotten?
CHESTER	Everything. Total blank.
CAROL	But I promised!
CHESTER	Did you?
CAROL	That's why I'm here.
CHESTER	I did wonder.
CAROL	I haven't forgotten, you see.
CHESTER	Haven't you?
CAROL	So when I heard that you'd arrived, naturally I came straight round.
CHESTER	Why?
CAROL	I was so excited I just had to come and say hullo.
CHESTER	Oh. Well – hullo.
CAROL	Hullo.

CHESTER   Well, that was hullo and this is goodbye.

                 (He takes her drink, puts it down on the table and
                 ushers her towards the door.)

CAROL   You wouldn't send me back in the rain?

CHESTER   Why not? You came here in the rain. Anyhow, it's
                 almost stopped.

CAROL   But I can't go out there like this. What would people
                 think?

CHESTER   Whatever they think it's all his fault.   (Indicating
                 the kitchen.)

CAROL   I'll have to wait until my dress dries.   (Moves to
                 D.L.C.)   Anyhow, I thought you'd be pleased to
                 see me.

CHESTER   Whatever gave you that idea?

CAROL   Well, I did keep my promise. So now I'm here why
                 don't we get on with it?

                 (CHESTER moves to R. of the sofa.)

CHESTER   Get on with what?

CAROL   With what you promised!

CHESTER   I didn't know I'd promised anything.

CAROL   That we'd be together.

                 (CHESTER goes to her quickly.)

CHESTER   I promised that?

CAROL   Six weeks ago. You said, 'When I come back we'll
                 always be together'.

CHESTER   I'm sure I'd have remembered.

CAROL   'The Horse and Groom'.

CHESTER   Were they there, too?

CAROL   That's where it was. 'The Horse and Groom'.

CHESTER   (a vague recollection)   Aaah –

CAROL   You do remember!

CHESTER   I seem to remember 'The Horse and Groom'. Very

	dark with lots of brass.
CAROL	You'd been looking at this house and you went for a few drinks and we got friendly in the saloon bar.
CHESTER	Not too friendly, I hope.
CAROL	You were very sweet -
CHESTER	(pleased) Was I? Oh, good!
CAROL	So you haven't forgotten me!
CHESTER	It was a very dark bar. I had a lot to drink. I remember that.
CAROL	Well, that's when it was.
CHESTER	When what was?
CAROL	When you said it.
CHESTER	'When I come back we'll always be together'?
CAROL	Yes.
CHESTER	You're sure I meant you?
CAROL	Well, I assumed you weren't referring to the landlord!
CHESTER	I might have been explaining -
CAROL	There was nothing to explain -
CHESTER	Explaining that when I came to live here I'd be together with my - er -
CAROL	You're not married?!
CHESTER	Aren't I?
CAROL	Don't tell me that!
CHESTER	Oh - er - Well, I -
CAROL	If you tell me that I'll - I'll -
	(A sudden rattle of gunfire a little distance away makes them both jump into each other's arms. She immediately enjoys being in his arms again.)
CHESTER	What the hell was that?
CAROL	(dreamily) Whatever it was, I'm glad it happened.
	(ABEL comes in.)

ABEL	You two at it again?
	(CHESTER disengages himself quickly and goes to ABEL.)
CHESTER	What was that noise?
ABEL	What noise?
CHESTER	Just now! You must have heard it!
ABEL	Ah - you mean the gunfire?
	(CHESTER looks aghast.)
CHESTER	Gunfire?
ABEL	That be it.
CHESTER	Don't be silly, Abel.
ABEL	That's what it was and how it is.
CHESTER	Gunfire?
ABEL	That's right.
CHESTER	Are we being invaded?
ABEL	Oh, no, sir.
CHESTER	Then what?
ABEL	It's down the road.
CHESTER	What's down the road?
ABEL	Where they learn how to do it.
CHESTER	(to CAROL) What's he talking about?
CAROL	The Army.
CHESTER	What?!
CAROL	There's a training camp just down the road.
CHESTER	Far down the road?
ABEL	Be about three hundred yards, I reckon.
CHESTER	But that's within rifle range!
ABEL	They won't be pointing in this direction.
CHESTER	They'd better not be. And this gunfire - does that happen very often?

(Another distant rattle of firearms. CAROL leaps
into CHESTER's arms again.)

ABEL   Got to practise now and then, haven't they?

CHESTER   Nobody told me that.   (He extricates himself.)

ABEL   You couldn't expect them not to practise, could you?

CHESTER   I mean I didn't know there was going to be an Army
                camp just down the road! Nobody told me that when
                I bought the place.

ABEL   Perhaps you never asked.

CHESTER   Why should I ask? When you go looking for a house
                you don't say, 'Oh, by the way, have you got an Army
                camp handy?'

ABEL   Didn't you hear the guns when you looked round?

CHESTER   It was Sunday, blast it!

ABEL   It's not always like this.

CHESTER   Isn't it?

ABEL   (heading for the kitchen)   No. Sometimes they go
                out on manoeuvres. Then you'll have a bit of peace.

CHESTER   Thank you very much.

                (ABEL disappears into the kitchen.)

                No wonder this place was empty for so long. And I
                thought I was getting a bargain.

CAROL   So you are. You're getting me!

CHESTER   That's something else I didn't know. Look, I've got
                to explain –

                (A car is heard pulling up and stopping outside.)

                Oh, my God! That'll be her!

CAROL   Who?

CHESTER   Oh – er – my –

CAROL   Mother?

CHESTER   Yes! My mother! You'd better go and get your dress
                on.

CAROL	It's still wet.
CHESTER	Well, you can't stay here like that! My mother might get the right idea.
CAROL	But I'd love to meet her.
CHESTER	Not like that. You'd better keep out of the way.
CAROL	Why?
CHESTER	Well – the thing is – she's very possessive. Still thinks I'm a little boy. That sort of thing. If she met you – like that – it would be the last straw. And she can be very angry when she's roused. Starts shouting all over the place.
CAROL	How awful!

(He urges her towards the stairs.)

CHESTER	Yes – so you keep out of the way. I'll tell you when it's all clear. Off you go!
CAROL	All right. But get rid of her quickly!
CHESTER	What?

(She goes off upstairs. He returns to C.)

Oh, my God – !

(The door opens and PATRICIA comes in. She is CHESTER's wife. She is about 35 and very attractive. She carries a suitcase and a bag of provisions.)

| PATRICIA | Darling! |

(She puts down her things U.R. and comes to him and embraces him. He is nervous and glances anxiously towards the stairs.)

What's the matter?

CHESTER	No!
PATRICIA	Is something wrong?
CHESTER	No – nothing at all!
PATRICIA	You don't seem very enthusiastic.

CHESTER   It's the rain. Very wet.

PATRICIA   I thought it was never going to stop. I could have
               been here much earlier.

CHESTER   Thank God you weren't!

PATRICIA   What?

CHESTER   You'd have got so wet. Getting out of the car.
               Running into the house. Very wet. Yes.

               (She looks around the room. It is fine now and the
               sun is starting to shine. She crosses to below the
               sofa.)

PATRICIA   So this is it.

CHESTER   What? Ah. The house. Yes. This is the house.
               We'll soon tidy up down here. Doesn't look very nice
               at the moment.

PATRICIA   I think it's lovely.

CHESTER   Do you? Good lord.

PATRICIA   Oh, I'd better go and help Mummy with the bags.

               (She starts to go but he intercepts her.)

CHESTER   Who?

PATRICIA   Mummy. I'd forgotten all about her.

CHESTER   So had I. Is she here?

PATRICIA   She's outside.

CHESTER   You didn't tell me she was coming!

PATRICIA   We wanted to surprise you.

CHESTER   Well, you have.

PATRICIA   She thought you could probably do with another pair of
               hands.

CHESTER   Oh, my God!

PATRICIA   There's no need to be rude.

CHESTER   I'm not being rude, darling. It's just that - well, I'd
               like to have got the place shipshape before your
               mother saw it.

PATRICIA   She likes to help.

CHESTER   (grimly)   Yes. I know she does. Well, I'll go and
                    help her with the bags.   (Goes out through the
                    front door.)

                    (PATRICIA sees the half-empty whisky bottle and two
                    glasses on the table. She picks up one, looks at it
                    briefly and puts it down again. She wanders to
                    D.L.C.   ABEL comes in from the kitchen and sees
                    her.)

ABEL   Well, I never. Now he's got another pair!

PATRICIA   I beg your pardon?

ABEL   That's three down here and one up there.

PATRICIA   Sorry?

ABEL   You just arrived?

PATRICIA   Yes.

ABEL   Stopped raining, has it?

PATRICIA   Yes.

ABEL   That's all right, then. You won't have to take your
                    dress off, will you?

                    (PATRICIA doesn't know what the hell he is talking
                    about. LADY ELROOD comes in from outside. She
                    is a well-dressed woman in her late fifties. She
                    sweeps in to C. and looks at the general untidiness.)

LADY E   Have we come to the wrong house?

PATRICIA   No, Mother.

LADY E   (in disbelief)   This is it?

PATRICIA   Yes.

LADY E   Good God –

                    (CHESTER comes in with two suitcases, and puts
                    them down wearily near the window seat R.)

CHESTER   What the hell have you got in here – lead weights?

LADY E   You didn't expect to see me arrive without any clothes?

CHESTER   No fear!

LADY E   I had to bring a _few_ things.

CHESTER   There's enough here to open a shop.   We shan't be changing for dinner, you know.   You could have left the tiaras at home.

PATRICIA   Chester –

LADY E   I came here to help.   And by the look of it I shall have my hands full.

ABEL   (muttering)   That's four down here and one up there –

LADY E   I beg your pardon?

CHESTER   This is Mr Bounty.

               (LADY ELROOD looks at him without enthusiasm.)

LADY E   How do you do, Mr Bounty.

CHESTER   Abel's here to help me.   Cleaning up and so on.

LADY E   You don't appear to have got very far.

ABEL   (crossing to behind the sofa)   You come and see upstairs, then.

               (PATRICIA eases to D. L.)

CHESTER   No!

LADY E   What?

CHESTER   (to R. of LADY ELROOD)   Not now.   You're tired.

LADY E   Am I?

CHESTER   Yes.   Tired after the journey.   Rain pouring down. Rattling on the roof.   Nothing worse.

LADY E   What's it like upstairs?

ABEL   (with a grin)   Very nice and pretty!

CHESTER   Abel –

ABEL   Very nice and clean.

LADY E   That's something.

ABEL   I had my wife over this morning.

CHESTER	Yes, Abel - we don't want all that again!
ABEL	(inexorably) We started in the bedroom -
CHESTER	(imitating his dialect) And carried on all morning. (He turns to LADY ELROOD.) He told me before. Abel, perhaps you'd take some of these things upstairs?
LADY E	And I'll come with you.
	(CHESTER goes quickly to her.)
CHESTER	No, you won't!
LADY E	What?
CHESTER	You can't start climbing up stairs without sitting down.
LADY E	I've been sitting down in the car.
CHESTER	This is much more comfortable. (He goes to below the sofa and moves some bits of newspaper and tidies it for her, causing the dust to fly a bit.)
	(LADY ELROOD comes D.C., watching CHESTER.)
LADY E	I can see that the sooner we get to work the better.
CHESTER	The kitchen! You'd rather see the kitchen. (To PATRICIA.) Wouldn't she?
PATRICIA	Well, I -
CHESTER	(to LADY E) There you are! You'd rather see the kitchen.
ABEL	Very tidy out there.
LADY E	I'm glad to hear it.
CHESTER	Very nice taps.
LADY E	Oh, very well. But then I shall see the upstairs.
ABEL	You don't have to worry, ma'am. The beds is made up nice and proper.
LADY E	That remains to be seen. (She sweeps off into the kitchen.)
ABEL	And I'll take these bags upstairs. (He collects CHESTER's suitcases from above the sofa.)

CHESTER   Oh, yes. If you would, Abel. And have a good look
               around, would you?

ABEL   (going)   Yes, sir.

CHESTER   Make sure the other luggage is out of the way.

ABEL   What?

CHESTER   You remember!

ABEL   Ah! Yes, sir. I will, sir. You bet, sir. Yes, sir.
               Right, sir.   (He goes with two cases, enjoying the
               situation.)

PATRICIA   Does he always get so excited about the luggage?

CHESTER   Well, he leads such a dull life, poor man. Only has
               to see a suitcase and he goes raving mad.

PATRICIA   (moving below him to the table)   Are you all
               right, darling?

CHESTER   Me? Never better. Why?

PATRICIA   You don't usually start drinking in the middle of the
               afternoon.

CHESTER   What?

               (She holds up the bottle.)

               Ah! Yes. Yes, I did have a small one. I'd
               forgotten. I got wet, you see. Very wet. Out there.
               So I thought a small sip would keep the cold out.

               (She looks at the level of the whisky.)

PATRICIA   I should think you're insulated for the winter after
               that.

CHESTER   Oh, I didn't drink all of it.

PATRICIA   I know you didn't.

CHESTER   As if I'd drink all that. Good heavens, no. What do
               you mean you know I didn't?

PATRICIA   There are two glasses here.   (She holds them up.)

               (He looks at them.)

CHESTER   Good lord, so there are. One, two. Yes, that's
               two all right.

PATRICIA	Well?
CHESTER	Yes.
PATRICIA	Yes, what?
CHESTER	Yes, please, I'd like another drink -
PATRICIA	Chester!
CHESTER	Yes, darling?
PATRICIA	Two glasses.
CHESTER	Ah, yes, of course - Abel!
PATRICIA	Who?
CHESTER	Abel Bounty. The luggage lunatic. It was him.
PATRICIA	The other glass?
CHESTER	Yes. That was his. He'd worked jolly hard all the morning so I thought he deserved a drink, so I gave him one. He was very pleased. Very grateful.
PATRICIA	Is that why he was wearing lipstick?
CHESTER	I beg your pardon?
PATRICIA	Lipstick.
CHESTER	Don't be silly, darling. Abel wouldn't wear lipstick. Not in the afternoon.
	(She holds one glass out to him. He looks at it.)
	That's lipstick all right.
PATRICIA	Perhaps you had a visitor.
CHESTER	(with a nervous laugh) Whatever gave you that idea?
PATRICIA	You seem to be in such a state.
CHESTER	Only because it was raining, and I hadn't got the place ready for you, and then your mother came and that was that.
PATRICIA	Perhaps you gave somebody else a drink?
CHESTER	What? Yes - that's right! Of course I did. I'd forgotten. Mrs Bounty.

PATRICIA	Sorry?
CHESTER	Abel's – thing – wife – you know!
PATRICIA	The one who started in the bedroom and carried on all morning?
CHESTER	That's right. Well, after that I thought, 'She deserves a drink'. So I gave her a large one.
	(A sudden rumble of gunfire. PATRICIA looks alarmed. CHESTER pretends not to notice.)
PATRICIA	Whatever was that?
CHESTER	What, darling?
PATRICIA	That noise.
CHESTER	I didn't hear anything.
PATRICIA	A sort of rumble.
CHESTER	Oh – that! Yes. Thunder. I expect it'll rain again in a minute.
PATRICIA	It didn't sound like thunder.
CHESTER	Didn't it? What a pity.
	(Another roll of gunfire in the distance.)
PATRICIA	There it is again!
	(LADY ELROOD comes out of the kitchen.)
LADY E	What on earth's going on?
CHESTER	There's nothing going on in <u>here</u>!
LADY E	Not in here! Out there!
CHESTER	In the kitchen?
LADY E	Down the road!
CHESTER	Yes.
LADY E	What do you mean 'Yes'? That's no answer.
CHESTER	Isn't it?
LADY E	Gunfire!
CHESTER	What?

LADY E	That's what it sounded like to me.
CHESTER	Yes.
LADY E	Don't keep saying 'Yes'!
CHESTER	No.
LADY E	What?
CHESTER	Sorry.
LADY E	(to PATRICIA) What about you? Gunfire?
PATRICIA	Definitely!
LADY E	That's what I thought. (To CHESTER.) Well? Is it or not?
CHESTER	I'd like to say not but it is.
LADY E	Gunfire?
CHESTER	Yes. That's what it was and how it is.
LADY E	You mean to tell me that what it was was gunfire?
CHESTER	Well, it was your suggestion.
LADY E	I was banking on denial!
CHESTER	Well, you won't get it here.
PATRICIA	Then it's true?
CHESTER	Yes. But a long way away.
LADY E	It sounded to me like three hundred yards.
CHESTER	Congratulations! First prize to you.
	(He offers her the whisky bottle which she waves aside.)
PATRICIA	Only three hundred yards away?
CHESTER	Yes. Army training camp.
PATRICIA	Oh, no!
LADY E	I knew you could never be trusted to buy a house on your own.
CHESTER	I thought you'd be pleased. It'll be like home-from-home. After all, your husband does a lot of shooting.

LADY E	Single shots do not a barrage make! I could never stay for long in a house with gunfire.
CHESTER	(pleased) Really? What a pity. I'd better leave your cases where they are, then.
PATRICIA	(fearfully) Does it go on all the time?
CHESTER	No, darling. Of course not. They'd soon run out of ammunition, wouldn't they? Sundays are very peaceful.
PATRICIA	That's something, I suppose – (ABEL comes downstairs. He moves to D.R. of them.)
CHESTER	Everything all right up there, Abel?
ABEL	Well, I took them up and put them down, but I can't keep the other up there for long.
LADY E	It sounds as if the bags have got a life of their own.
CHESTER	Yes, you could say that. There's no room up there. That's what you meant, wasn't it, Abel?
ABEL	That's right, sir. (To LADY E.) Wouldn't like you to go up there and find the baggage all over the place.
CHESTER	Has it – dried off all right?
ABEL	Not quite.
CHESTER	(to LADY E) One of them got awfully wet in the rain.
LADY E	Why didn't you rub it all over with a towel?
CHESTER	I never thought of that. (To ABEL.) How long do you think, Abel?
ABEL	Any minute now, I should think.
CHESTER	Oh, my God!
LADY E	(to ABEL) Mr Bounty, would you go and put the kettle on? I'm dying for tea.
ABEL	Right you are. (He goes below them to the kitchen, chuckling.) Any minute now, there'll be five down

here and none up there –   (He goes out.)

(CHESTER goes to pick up the cases from near the window seat.)

CHESTER   I'll put these back in the car.

PATRICIA   (moving to R. of the sofa)   Darling, you've only just brought them in.

CHESTER   I know. But they don't like it and they want to go.

PATRICIA   What are you talking about?

CHESTER   Your mother and these – and you and yours – back in the car!

PATRICIA   Back in the car?

CHESTER   Back in the car and off!

PATRICIA   Off where?

CHESTER   Out of earshot. I can't have you sleeping here with gunfire.

PATRICIA   I'll get used to it.

LADY E   Earplugs!

CHESTER   What?

LADY E   She can wear earplugs if it gets too bad.

PATRICIA   Of course. And after a couple of weeks we won't even notice.

CHESTER   Won't we?

PATRICIA   (smiling warmly)   After two weeks I won't notice anything.

CHESTER   I wish I could be sure of that. Anyway, you're here and I'm ready. Come along, you go to the village and wait.   (He starts to go.)

PATRICIA   The village and wait?

CHESTER   I'll call you when I've sorted everything out here. Look at all this mess. It's too much and I can't have more.

PATRICIA   (following him a little)   But that's what we came for. Mummy and I came to lend a hand.

CHESTER   We've got enough of those already. I'll tell you when
              it's all clear.

PATRICIA   All clear?

CHESTER   All clean! Spick and span. Bright and shiny. So
              come on - into the car - off to the village and wait.
              You can find a nice hotel and stay there -

LADY E   'The Horse and Groom'?

CHESTER   (guiltily)   What do you know about that?

LADY E   We stopped there on the way.

PATRICIA   And dropped Daddy off.

CHESTER   What?

PATRICIA   We left him there. He had a few things to see to.
              Said he'd come on later.

              (CHESTER puts down the cases U.R. and turns to her.)

CHESTER   You mean your father's coming here as well?

PATRICIA   Yes, of course.

CHESTER   Oh, no - !

PATRICIA   Well, after all, we don't move into a new house every
              day.

CHESTER   Thank God for that! Still, if he's already there, you
              can both go to the village and wait with him.

LADY E   Nonsense! We're staying here. There's a lot to do.
              (She heads for the kitchen.)

PATRICIA   (embracing him)   Yes, of course we are, darling.
              After all - this is my home now.

CHESTER   Is it? Oh, lord -

LADY E   (going)   Mr Bounty! What's happening to the tea?
              (She goes into the kitchen.)

PATRICIA   I'm sorry, darling.

CHESTER   What?

PATRICIA   Bringing Mummy and Daddy along. I couldn't stop
              them. But they do mean well. They only want to help.

(Arm-in-arm, they wander to R. of the sofa.)

CHESTER Yes. I know that, darling. It's just that - well, your mother's one thing - but your father does take a bit of getting used to.

PATRICIA What do you mean?

CHESTER You know what he's like at home!

PATRICIA Full of high spirits.

CHESTER They've all got used to him by now, but here - nobody knows us yet, and - well, they might think it a bit odd if he starts shooting at the postman.

PATRICIA Well, you'll just have to warn him.

CHESTER Your father?

PATRICIA The postman!

(LADY ELROOD returns.)

LADY E You didn't remember to order gas, I suppose?

CHESTER Gas?

LADY E It comes out of a pipe.

CHESTER It was there yesterday. It can't have gone far.

LADY E Well, Mr Bounty seems to be struggling.

CHESTER Oh, for heaven's sake! I'll see to it!

(He goes off with LADY ELROOD to the kitchen. PATRICIA goes to sort out some of the luggage and so has her back to the stairs and does not see CAROL coming down. CAROL is now wearing a man's shirt and trousers. The trousers are rolled up at the ankle as they are a bit long for her.)

CAROL Can I come down now?

(PATRICIA turns and sees a pretty girl in a man's shirt and trousers, and is - not surprisingly - surprised.)

PATRICIA Oh - er - yes. I suppose so.

(CAROL comes to PATRICIA and holds out her hand. PATRICIA is puzzled and suspicious, CAROL

	friendly and smiling. They meet U. R. C.)
CAROL	How do you do.
PATRICIA	Oh - how do you do.
CAROL	You got here all right, then?
PATRICIA	Yes, thank you.
CAROL	You look quite dry. You must have missed the rain.
PATRICIA	It had stopped before we got out of the car.
CAROL	Lucky for you.
PATRICIA	Yes. It was, wasn't it?
CAROL	I got soaked.
PATRICIA	Really?
CAROL	That's why I'm dressed like this.
PATRICIA	I did wonder.
	(A pause.)
CAROL	My dress is upstairs. I took it off in the bedroom.
PATRICIA	That's as good a place as anywhere else.
CAROL	Sorry?
PATRICIA	Never mind.
CAROL	It's a super bedroom.
PATRICIA	Is it really?
CAROL	Super!
PATRICIA	Perhaps I shall see it one day.
CAROL	Any time you like.
PATRICIA	Thank you very much. (Puzzled, she moves to below the sofa.)
	(A pause. CAROL comes down to R. of the sofa.)
CAROL	These aren't my clothes, of course.
PATRICIA	I didn't think they were somehow.
CAROL	My clothes fit better than these.

PATRICIA	Yes. I bet they do.
	(A pause.)
CAROL	They're his.
PATRICIA	Sorry?
CAROL	His clothes. I found them in the bedroom.
PATRICIA	I thought they looked familiar.
CAROL	I've been unpacking for him.
PATRICIA	How very kind.
	(CAROL moves to below the table.)
CAROL	I say – I hope you don't mind my saying this –
PATRICIA	Please feel free. Say anything you like.
CAROL	Well – you're much younger than I expected.
PATRICIA	(coldly) Am I really?
CAROL	I mean – you don't look all that much older than I do.
PATRICIA	Thank you very much.
CAROL	I suppose you've looked after yourself.
PATRICIA	Well, I've tried. A face-lift here and a hormone there. Why on earth should you think I was going to be older?
CAROL	Because of what he told me.
PATRICIA	Chester?
CAROL	Yes.
PATRICIA	He told you I'd be older?
CAROL	Not exactly. I just assumed you would be. From what he said about you.
PATRICIA	I see –
	(And if PATRICIA could see CHESTER now, looks would undoubtedly kill.)
CAROL	Oh, dear. You're not angry, are you?
	(PATRICIA smiles. But not with her eyes.)

PATRICIA   No, no. Of course I'm not angry.   (She glances towards the kitchen.)   Not yet.

CAROL   I couldn't bear it if you started shouting.

PATRICIA   Then I must try hard to control myself, mustn't I?

CAROL   (considerately)   It's so much better if you don't, you know. You should try counting to ten, and then you probably wouldn't want to shout at all.

              (CHESTER comes in from the kitchen, angrily.)

CHESTER   I can't turn that bloody gas on -   (He stops as he sees CAROL in his clothes.)   Oh, my God!
              (He turns to go back again.)

PATRICIA   Chester!

              (He stops nervously.)

CHESTER   Yes, dear?

PATRICIA   Do come and join us. We're having such an interesting conversation.

CHESTER   I thought you might be. You've - er - introduced yourselves, I suppose?

PATRICIA   Not exactly.

CHESTER   That's all right, then.

              (He takes a deep breath and crosses to CAROL, expansively.)

              Well - what a lovely surprise! You were able to come back after all, then, Mrs Bounty!

              (The girls react. PATRICIA moves to his L.; CAROL to his R.)

PATRICIA   What?

CAROL   What are you talking about?

CHESTER   We didn't think you'd be able to come back this afternoon.   (Pointedly to CAROL.)   Did we, Mrs Bounty?

              (CAROL is bewildered.)

CAROL   Didn't we?

CHESTER	No, of course we didn't!
CAROL	But I'm not –
CHESTER	Tired? Not tired? You must be after all your hard work this morning. That's why it's so good of you to come back and finish off this afternoon. (To PATRICIA.) Isn't it? Yes, of course it is. And we're very grateful. (To PATRICIA.) Aren't we? Yes, of course we are. Why don't you go and finish off upstairs?
PATRICIA	She's only just come down.
CHESTER	Oh, I see! You've finished upstairs?
PATRICIA	Yes. She's even unpacked your case. Wasn't that sweet of her?
CHESTER	I thought I recognised that shirt. And those trousers! I say, you mustn't let old Bounty see you in those. He might get the wrong idea, eh? (He laughs nervously.)
	(PATRICIA may well accept CAROL as MRS BOUNTY, unlikely as it may seem, but she is still seething over what CHESTER said about her.)
PATRICIA	(coldly) I think I'd like to go and have a look upstairs now. (She crosses below them on her way to the stairs.)
CHESTER	What a good idea!
PATRICIA	Then Mrs Bounty can carry on down here.
CAROL	Yes – rather! (She smiles at CHESTER.)
CHESTER	(to PATRICIA) Shall I come and show you the way?
PATRICIA	No, thank you. I think I can manage. My eyesight's still quite good – considering my age. (She goes to the stairs.)
CHESTER	What? Oh – all right. You go ahead and I'll have a drink – I mean, you go ahead and I'll have a go at the gas.
PATRICIA	I'm so looking forward to seeing the bedroom. I've heard so much about it.

(She goes off upstairs. CHESTER turns back to CAROL.)

CHESTER — I told you to stay upstairs.

CAROL — I couldn't stay there for ever.

CHESTER — And what are you doing with my clothes on? What will people think? You'd better take them off.

CAROL — All right. (She proceeds to take the shirt off.)

CHESTER — Not now! (He helps her back into it.)

CAROL — Well, make up your mind.

CHESTER — What have you been saying to her? She looked awfully cross.

CAROL — (innocently) Nothing. We had a nice little chat. You never told me she was so young.

CHESTER — I think I'd better go and speak to her.

CAROL — Never mind her. What about me?

CHESTER — You can't stay here. That dress must be dry by now. Put it on and pop off.

CAROL — Why did you tell her I was Mrs Bounty?

CHESTER — Because she doesn't know about you!

CAROL — You'll have to tell her sooner or later.

(A rattle of gunfire from down the road. She leaps into his arms and he is holding her when LADY ELROOD comes in from the kitchen and reacts to what she sees.)

LADY E — Chester!

(CHESTER and CAROL spring apart.)

What is going on?

CHESTER — Gunfire!

LADY E — Not out there. In here.

CHESTER — Yes.

LADY E — Don't start saying 'Yes' again!

CHESTER	No.
LADY E	What?
CHESTER	Sorry.
LADY E	Well?
CHESTER	She's very nervous. (To CAROL.) Aren't you? Yes. So I was looking after her. The guns went bang and she jumped and I was - er -
LADY E	I saw what you were doing!
CHESTER	Did you? Well, it probably looked better than it was. Worse than it was. Gunfire does funny things to people.
LADY E	Mr Bounty and I were in the kitchen when the guns rolled. We did not leap into each other's arms.
CHESTER	What a pity. You'd have liked that.
LADY E	What?!
CHESTER	Let me introduce you. (He goes to R. of CAROL.) This is - er - this is Mrs Bounty.
LADY E	(surprised) Mr Bounty's wife?
CHESTER	The very same.
LADY E	Don't be ridiculous.
CHESTER	Unlikely but true.
LADY E	This Mr Bounty?
CHESTER	Yes.
LADY E	Good heavens. (She crosses to CAROL.) How do you do, Mrs Bounty.
CAROL	Oh, I'm not really -
	(CHESTER pushes her and gives her a look. She decides to go along with it.)
	How do you do.
LADY E	I hear you're quite an expert in the bedrooms.
CAROL	I do my best. (She giggles modestly.)
	(CHESTER feels embarrassed and gives a little cough.)

CHESTER	Cleaning! Yes. They did awfully well. Both of them.
CAROL	(to LADY E, puzzled) When did <u>you</u> arrive, then?
LADY E	A few minutes ago. I came with my daughter.
CAROL	Your daughter?
LADY E	Patricia. She was here a moment ago.
CAROL	(realising) Oh, I see! Good heavens! So <u>you're</u> his mother?
LADY E	What?
CAROL	Oh, dear. That means <u>she</u> must be - How awful of me!
LADY E	(to CHESTER) What's she talking about?
CHESTER	I don't know. Would you like to see the upstairs now?
LADY E	I hope it's better than the downstairs.
CHESTER	You go first and I'll follow.
	(LADY ELROOD goes to the stairs.)
LADY E	Will you be staying for long, Mrs Bounty?
CAROL	Well, I -
CHESTER	No! (Going towards the stairs.) She has to go home. Got to cook the dinner. Hasn't done the sprouts yet.
CAROL	I can't go home without my dress on.
LADY E	What's that?
CAROL	I took it off in the bedroom.
	(LADY ELROOD goes off upstairs, not quite sure what to make of it all. CHESTER hangs back.)
	You're not a bit <u>like</u> her, are you?
CHESTER	I hope not! Look, you can go in my shirt and things. You can't stay here. Not now they're here.
CAROL	But why not?
LADY E	(off) Chester!

CHESTER   (calling)   Coming!   (To CAROL.)   Look - I'm
                 going upstairs now, and when I come back you'd better
                 be gone.

                 (He starts to go. CAROL moves towards him.)

CAROL   Well, I think it's very sweet.

CHESTER   What is?

CAROL   Your mother and your sister both coming to help you.

CHESTER   What?   (He goes off, bewildered.)

                 (CAROL moves down to the fireplace as the front
                 door creaks open and MISS PARTRIDGE wanders in.
                 She is a somewhat eccentric woman of about 50. She
                 wears tweeds, beads and carries a capacious
                 handbag. She walks in to R.C. looking about the
                 place with delight. CAROL watches in surprise.)

MISS P   So this is the place! I've heard so much about it.

CAROL   Really?

MISS P   Oh, yes. You couldn't keep a place like this a secret
                 from me for long. Oh, no! Just look at those beams!
                 (She looks enraptured at the beams.)

                 (CAROL moves to below the sofa.)

CAROL   Are you looking for something?

MISS P   I always am, my dear.

CAROL   Well - can I help you?

MISS P   That depends.   (She goes to CAROL.)   Do you
                 know any history?

CAROL   Not a lot.

MISS P   Ever studied Roman remains?

CAROL   Can't say I have.

MISS P   Fossils?

CAROL   I saw one at the seaside!

MISS P   You're not a student of archaeology?

CAROL   Oh, no.

MISS P	You've got a man's shirt on.
CAROL	Yes.
MISS P	Extraordinary - (She moves on, looking about the room.) Just look at that fireplace.
CAROL	Yes. I'm sorry about that. We haven't had time to do down here yet.
MISS P	If you stand here and breathe in deeply -
CAROL	I wouldn't do that. It's very dusty.
MISS P	You can sense the tang of the fourteenth century.
CAROL	Really?
MISS P	The minute I came in here I felt the atmosphere. Such history!
	(A rattle of gunfire. MISS PARTRIDGE goes to L. of CAROL.)
	Did you hear that? Echoes of the past!
CAROL	No. Gunfire down the road.
MISS P	I can see you're not in tune with the Middle Ages.
CAROL	I'm afraid not.
MISS P	I'm rather surprised to find you here. I was told this house was empty, that nobody would buy it. Places so steeped in history often remain empty, you know.
CAROL	Oh, it wasn't that. It was gunfire.
MISS P	Gunfire?
CAROL	The Army.
MISS P	I hope they're not coming here!
CAROL	Oh, no.
MISS P	We can't have that! Heavy-footed soldiers disturbing the vibrations of the past. We must prevent them at all costs. A man's trousers, as well.
CAROL	Oh - yes.
MISS P	Any particular reason?

CAROL	It's a long story.
MISS P	I'm sure it is. (Moves below CAROL to D.C.) If these walls could only speak!

(ABEL comes in from the kitchen with a tray on which are some mugs of tea.)

ABEL	I've had to make the tea on an old primus stove. (Sees MISS PARTRIDGE.) What's this then? Another pair of hands?
MISS P	Partridge!
ABEL	Wrong time of the year for them.
MISS P	No, no! That's my name.
ABEL	Partridge?
MISS P	That's right. Miss Partridge. Are you the new owner?
ABEL	No fear. I'd never buy a place like this. I'm just here to help out.

(MISS PARTRIDGE moves U.S., looking about.)

MISS P	There's magic in this building!
ABEL	There's dry rot, an' all.

(CAROL goes to ABEL and takes a mug of tea.)

MISS P	Can't you feel the atmosphere? It transports you from the present and plunges you back into the past!
ABEL	Well, I dunno about the building, but that gas cooker's a bit of a relic, I can tell you.
MISS P	You don't suppose the owner will mind, do you?
ABEL	Mind what?
MISS P	My being here.
ABEL	He probably won't notice. He's got his hands full already.
MISS P	Just look at that roof!

(ABEL looks up, alarmed.)

ABEL	Not coming down, is it?

MISS P	And listen to this.
	(She gets a small mallet out of her bag and goes towards the staircase. ABEL and CAROL exchange a look. Who is this crazy woman? MISS PARTRIDGE taps with her mallet on the banisters. ABEL goes up behind the sofa to L. of MISS PARTRIDGE. CAROL eases D. L.)
ABEL	I wouldn't do that if I were you. There's them upstairs as might not get down.
MISS P	Did you hear that? It has the ring of antiquity! (Moving D. C.) I shall spend some fascinating hours here, I can tell you.
ABEL	Does that mean you'll be staying, then?
MISS P	I can't leave this place now. Standing here I can feel history throbbing in my veins.
ABEL	Well, I wouldn't stand there throbbing too long, 'cos that's where the dry rot started.
	(MISS PARTRIDGE is wandering enraptured towards the kitchen.)
MISS P	It was fate that brought me here, you know. I was drawn here inexorably. I mustn't waste one single minute. The very bricks are alive with a sense of the past! (She goes off into the kitchen.)
ABEL	(moving to above the sofa) Where'd you find her, then?
CAROL	She just walked straight in.
ABEL	Well, p'raps you better go and keep an eye on her before she walks straight out with the silver.
CAROL	You think she might do that?
ABEL	You never know with people like her. Might not be as daft as she makes out. You've got a man's shirt on.
CAROL	I know that! (She goes out to the kitchen.)
	(ABEL shrugs, unable to make out what is going on, and makes for the stairs with his tray of tea. CHESTER returns, sees that CAROL is not there

and looks relieved.)

CHESTER   That's a relief!

ABEL   Yes, I thought you'd be glad of it.

CHESTER   What?

ABEL   Tea!

CHESTER   Oh - thank you, Abel.   (Takes a mug of tea.)
           You got it working all right, then?

ABEL   Oh, no. I fell back on my primus.

CHESTER   Good heavens! Like being branded.

ABEL   Oh, I wasn't on the primus, sir.

CHESTER   I thought you said -

ABEL   It was the kettle that was on the primus.

CHESTER   Oh, I see. What about the cooker?

ABEL   Can't get it started. It's stuck for good, that's
           what, so that's that.

CHESTER   Stuck for good and that's that?

ABEL   Right.

CHESTER   You'll have to get a man in from the village.

ABEL   Eh?

CHESTER   There's a man in the village, isn't there? Well,
           you'll have to get him in.

ABEL   Right you are, sir. First thing in the morning.

CHESTER   We can't have you falling back on your primus all
           the time.   (Moves below ABEL to R.C.)
           Well - she's gone all right, then?

ABEL   I hope so, sir.

CHESTER   Pity, in a way. Such a pretty little thing.

           (ABEL looks puzzled. He comes D. S. a little.)

ABEL   Eh?

CHESTER   Didn't you think so?

ABEL   Reckon I've seen better.

CHESTER   Lucky for you. Did you lend her a coat to go in?

ABEL   She didn't seem interested. Not in clothes, sir.

CHESTER   (smiling)   No, she didn't, did she?

ABEL   Just stood over there, breathing heavy and throbbing
                 a bit.

CHESTER   Throbbing a bit?

ABEL   That's right.

CHESTER   Poor little thing. She <u>must</u> have been upset. I
                 suppose I did treat her badly.

ABEL   (at a loss)   I'd better go take them their tea.

CHESTER   If you can get in. They locked me out.

ABEL   Like that, is it?

CHESTER   You can never please a woman, Abel.

ABEL   Well, I don't know about that, sir -

CHESTER   Abel!

ABEL   Sorry, sir.   (He nods his head towards the stairs.)
                 That's the pair of hands you said was coming on
                 later, I take it?

CHESTER   Yes. That's right. Only she wasn't late enough.

ABEL   How about the other?

CHESTER   I didn't know <u>she</u> was coming at all!

ABEL   Life's full of surprises, isn't it? Still, you've got
                 plenty of ladies now to help you tidy up.

CHESTER   Too many.

ABEL   Yes - two up there and two down here!   (He goes
                 off upstairs.)

                 (CHESTER looks puzzled for a moment, then shrugs
                 it off as an error in ABEL's arithmetic. He takes a
                 swig of tea without thinking. It is horrible - and
                 cold. He splutters, puts down the mug of tea and
                 reaches quickly for the whisky bottle. As he opens it
                 there is a loud bang from a gun outside. He jumps.)

CHESTER   Good heavens!

(He pours a large whisky. There is a second shot. He takes a large gulp of whisky. LORD ELROOD comes in from outside, beaming with pleasure. He is in his early sixties, a game old war-horse. He is dressed in country tweeds and carries a shotgun. He moves to R. of CHESTER.)

ELROOD   I gave the blighters a couple of quick blasts! That should keep their heads down for a bit.

CHESTER   Yes. I'm sure it will.

ELROOD   You drinking on duty?

CHESTER   (patiently)   Father – it's me!

ELROOD   What?

CHESTER   Your son-in-law!

ELROOD   Well, what the hell made you choose this place? (He goes to the window seat R.)

CHESTER   Now don't you start!

ELROOD   Too much cover. They could creep up and surround us in no time.   (Looking out of the window.) Just look at that.

CHESTER   You must remember you're not at home now.

ELROOD   (not paying attention)   What's that?

CHESTER   (crossing to him)   You'll have to behave. It's all very well taking a pot shot at the postman at home – he's learned to live with it – but here it's different.

ELROOD   (not having heard)   It certainly is. The defences are appalling.

                (CAROL comes in from the kitchen.)

CAROL   Whatever's going on?

                (CHESTER looks alarmed.)

CHESTER   I thought you'd gone!

CAROL   I heard shooting.

ELROOD   (seeing her and moving to R. of the sofa)   Good God! What's this? They're not calling up women already, are they?

CAROL   (to CHESTER)   What's he talking about?

ELROOD   Name, rank and number!

CAROL   Eh?

CHESTER   She's not in the Army.

ELROOD   She's wearing a man's shirt.

CAROL   I know!

CHESTER   It's mine.

ELROOD   Share and share alike, eh? Good man. That's the
                  spirit I like to see. What's your name?

CAROL   (quickly)   Carol!

                  (ELROOD peers at her.)

ELROOD   (to CHESTER)   Not the same one you had before,
                  is it?

CHESTER   Er - no.

ELROOD   Well, I'm sure we can find a place for her.

CAROL   Is that thing loaded?

ELROOD   (chuckling)   Not any more!   (He goes back to
                  the window.)

CAROL   What's he doing here?

CHESTER   (R. of the sofa)   I think he's come for the shooting.

CAROL   What?

CHESTER   I dunno. Partridge, I suppose.

CAROL   Oh, no! Partridge?

CHESTER   Why not?

CAROL   She's not as bad as all that!

CHESTER   (moving to below the sofa)   What are you talking
                  about?

CAROL   Perhaps I had better go and keep an eye on the silver,
                  then.   (She makes for the kitchen.)

                  (ELROOD turns from the window.)

ELROOD   Did I give you permission to leave?

CAROL	Sorry?
ELROOD	Discipline. Got to have discipline, remember.
CAROL	I was only going to the kitchen.
ELROOD	Check the rations, eh? Very well. Permission granted. Carry on!
CAROL	Thank you. (She looks puzzled at CHESTER and starts to go.)
ELROOD	See you on the battlements tonight.
	(CAROL reacts and goes. ELROOD watches her go, appreciatively.)
	H'm. Not bad. I'd like to see her in a tight corner.
CHESTER	Yes, so would I!
ELROOD	I should think she'd put up quite a bit of a fight.
CHESTER	I wouldn't be too sure.
	(LADY ELROOD comes downstairs to C.)
LADY E	Oh, hullo, dear. I thought I heard you arriving.
ELROOD	Always take the fight to the enemy!
LADY E	(who has heard it all before) Yes, dear. (To CHESTER.) Do you think you could tell Mr Bounty to stop wandering about with mugs of cold tea? (To ELROOD.) We're having dreadful trouble with our pipes.
CHESTER	Abel's fallen back on his primus.
LADY E	I don't think we want to hear about that, thank you very much.
CHESTER	He was only trying to help.
LADY E	The result was cold tea.
CHESTER	He's getting a man from the village.
LADY E	I'm sure we shall all be glad of that.
ELROOD	Everything as it should be up there?
LADY E	Yes, dear. I think so. (Looking at CHESTER.) I'm not so sure about down here.

ELROOD   As soon as it's dark we'll have to mount guard.

LADY E   Yes. That'll be lovely. We weren't expecting you
             quite so soon. Didn't you like it at 'The Horse and
             Groom'?

ELROOD   Didn't fancy the quarters. Wasn't made very welcome.

LADY E   Oh, dear. Why not?

ELROOD   I took a pot shot at the porter. They didn't seem to
             like it.

LADY E   Well, it does take a bit of getting used to. It was the
             uniform, I suppose.   (Moving to R. of CHESTER.)
             He gets very confused over uniform. Does tend to
             mix up military with civil. The postman simply
             refuses to come to our place any more.

CHESTER   I don't blame him.

LADY E   The letters get delivered with the meat. The
             butcher's much better at using the cover.

             (ABEL comes downstairs with the tray of mugs. He
             moves to C.)

ABEL   I made my tea and now nobody wants it.   (Seeing
             ELROOD.)   I thought I heard shots.

             (ELROOD sees him and brings his gun up to the ready.)

ELROOD   Stay where you are!

             (ABEL looks alarmed as he finds a shotgun thrust
             into his stomach.)

ABEL   Here! You go easy with that now.

ELROOD   Put 'em up!

ABEL   What?

ELROOD   Put 'em up! Put 'em up!

ABEL   I'll drop this lot if I do.

CHESTER   It's all right. This is Mr Bounty. He's with us.

ELROOD   I see.

ABEL   You wouldn't like a cup of cold tea, I suppose?

ELROOD   No, thanks. I'll have some cocoa with the men later.

ABEL	Don't tell me there's some more arriving? I wonder if you'd mind pointing that thing somewhere else, sir?
ELROOD	Oh - yes - rather. (Lowers the gun.) Always got to be sure, though. You're in charge of catering, then?
ABEL	Eh?
CHESTER	Yes - that's right. He's the Cook Sergeant.
ELROOD	Capital! Then why aren't you in uniform?
ABEL	(to CHESTER) What's he talking about? I haven't been in uniform since 1945.
LADY E	Don't pay any attention. He's my husband.
ABEL	Oh, I _am_ sorry.
LADY E	He's always longing for the old days.
ABEL	I can see that. Shall I make some more tea?
LADY E	No, thank you, Mr Bounty. It's kind of you, but I really don't think we can risk you falling back on your primus again so soon.
ELROOD	I'd better go and examine the arcs of fire. You'll be on guard tonight, of course, sergeant?
CHESTER	(to ABEL) I think he's talking to you.
ABEL	What's that, sir?
ELROOD	Guard duty tonight!
ABEL	Well, I _was_ going home to the wife, sir.
ELROOD	Out of the question. All weekend leave is cancelled indefinitely! (He goes off upstairs.)
	(CHESTER grins at ABEL.)
CHESTER	You'll get used to him in time.
ABEL	(moving D.C.) I hope he doesn't really expect me to stay here. I promised the wife, see?
LADY E	Of course you did, Mr Bounty. And I can quite understand you wanting to get home to her.
ABEL	(ruefully) Yes. If I don't I'll be in trouble.

LADY E	You're a lucky man.
ABEL	(surprised) I am?
LADY E	She's very pretty.
ABEL	My wife?
LADY E	Yes.
ABEL	You call that pretty?
LADY E	You obviously don't appreciate her.
ABEL	I'll have another look when I get home. But I didn't know you'd seen her.
LADY E	Oh, yes. We've seen her all right. Haven't we, Chester? You had a good look, didn't you?
CHESTER	What?
LADY E	Mrs Bounty.
CHESTER	Oh, yes - rather! We've seen her. Very pretty.
LADY E	She was here.
ABEL	(puzzled) But mine went out before yours came in.
CHESTER	Ah - yes - but yours came back again.
ABEL	I didn't know that.
CHESTER	You were out there fiddling with your primus.
ABEL	I never heard nothing.
CHESTER	She was very quiet. Wasn't she? Yes. Like a mouse. Didn't want to disturb you.
ABEL	Why not?
CHESTER	She thought you might be cross. I mean, you were here thinking she was there seeing to the sprouts, and all the time she was here seeing to us.
ABEL	Why'd she come back, then?
CHESTER	You keep asking questions. No wonder the tea was cold. She came to help.
ABEL	She helped this morning.
CHESTER	Yes, I know, but she enjoyed carrying on upstairs so

much that she came back to carry on down here.

ABEL   Well, I don't see her anywhere.

CHESTER   No. She's gone home.

ABEL   Hardly seems worth her while to have come back, then.

CHESTER   I expect she came to put her dress on.

(The sound of a shotgun from upstairs.)

ABEL   Here! He's firing that thing again! (Making for the kitchen.) I'm going to get off home while I'm still in one piece! (He dashes off into the kitchen.)

(PATRICIA races on from upstairs. She carries CAROL's dressing-gown and a small suitcase. She comes to R. of the sofa.)

PATRICIA   Mummy, you'll have to speak to him!

LADY E   You know he never takes any notice of me.

PATRICIA   Well, he'll have to! He's just taken a pot shot at the paper boy.

CHESTER   Now, instead of reading the news we shall be in it.

LADY E   Did he hit him?

PATRICIA   Luckily, no. The boy was far too quick.

LADY E   Oh, dear. He does get so depressed when he misses.

PATRICIA   Mummy! We have only just moved in and already we haven't got a paper boy!

LADY E   There's no need to raise your voice. (She goes up the stairs.)

PATRICIA   Then will you please tell him to stop?

LADY E   All right. All right. I'm going. I knew you should never have bought a house in the country. (And with this non sequitur she disappears upstairs.)

(CHESTER is aware of PATRICIA's eye on him, and also of the dressing-gown she is carrying. He smiles feebly.)

CHESTER   Going somewhere, darling?

	(She holds out the dressing-gown.)
PATRICIA	I found this in our bedroom!
CHESTER	It's mine.
PATRICIA	What?!
CHESTER	I mean - it's not mine. Not my size. Far too small.
PATRICIA	Then whose?
CHESTER	Yes.
PATRICIA	Don't keep saying 'Yes'.
CHESTER	No.
PATRICIA	What?
CHESTER	Sorry.
PATRICIA	Well?
CHESTER	It belongs to my sister.
PATRICIA	You expect me to believe that?
CHESTER	No, but I couldn't think of anything else.
PATRICIA	Perhaps it belongs to Mrs Bounty?
CHESTER	Don't be silly, darling. Why should Mrs Bounty want to bring her dressing-gown?
PATRICIA	Perhaps because she was going to take her clothes off.
CHESTER	Yes, but she didn't know that.
PATRICIA	What?!
CHESTER	That it was going to rain! Anyhow, there was no need for her to bring that. I lent her some of mine. No, I shouldn't have said that.
PATRICIA	Why not?
CHESTER	It doesn't help me.
PATRICIA	Has she gone?
CHESTER	Mrs Bounty? Yes. She went that way.
PATRICIA	Well, she's left her case behind. (Puts the suitcase on the sofa table.)

CHESTER	I bet I know where you found that. In our bedroom!
PATRICIA	Yes.
CHESTER	It's mine!
PATRICIA	Are you sure?
CHESTE R	Absolutely positive.
	(PATRICIA opens the case and takes out a frivolous nightie.)
PATRICIA	I didn't know you'd started wearing one of these.
	(He remains quite still for a moment, stunned.)
CHESTER	There's been a dreadful mistake.
PATRICIA	Yes. And it's all _yours_!
CHESTER	It belongs to my sister.
PATRICIA	Not _her_ again!
CHESTER	I went to see her on my-way down here. You know how it is. Family feeling. In the area – stop and say hullo. So I did.
PATRICIA	And stayed the night?
CHESTER	Yes.
PATRICIA	With your suitcase?
CHESTER	With my suitcase with my sister. It all happened last Christmas.
PATRICIA	I thought you said it happened last night?
CHESTER	It was last Christmas that mother gave both of us a present.
PATRICIA	I see –
CHESTER	She gave us both – a suitcase! Wasn't that kind?
PATRICIA	Very kind.
CHESTER	That's what _I_ thought.
PATRICIA	And they both looked exactly the same?
CHESTER	How ever did you guess?

PATRICIA   I just had that feeling.

CHESTER   Well, when I left – early – in a hurry – I took the
                wrong one. So I've got this, and she's sleeping in
                my pyjamas.

                (PATRICIA smiles unexpectedly and moves in close
                to CHESTER. He is somewhat surprised.)

PATRICIA   Darling –

CHESTER   H'm?

PATRICIA   Aren't you going to put your arms around me?

CHESTER   Oh. All right.

                (He embraces her nervously and not too well.)

PATRICIA   Go on. You can do better than that.

CHESTER   Can I? Oh – right.   (He does a little better.)

PATRICIA   Poor you.

CHESTER   Sorry?

PATRICIA   Leaving your suitcase behind like that.

CHESTER   You mean you believe me?

PATRICIA   Yes, of course.

CHESTER   Good lord –   (So he does a little better still.)

                (PATRICIA gently draws away from him, gives him a
                little kiss and goes towards the stairs.)

                Where are you going?

PATRICIA   I'd better look up the 'phone number, hadn't I?

CHESTER   What 'phone number?

PATRICIA   Your sister's, of course. She'll want to know what's
                happened to her suitcase, won't she?

                (And with the smallest hint of a twinkle she goes off
                upstairs. CHESTER realises he is by no means out
                of trouble, sees the whisky and makes for it. As he
                does so, the front door opens abruptly and an
                Army SERGEANT bursts in. He is about 35, a
                forceful Cockney. CHESTER looks at him in wonder.)

SERGEANT	Right! Who are you?
CHESTER	I beg your pardon.
SERGEANT	What you doing 'ere?
CHESTER	I live here!
SERGEANT	Not yesterday.
CHESTER	What?
SERGEANT	You didn't live 'ere yesterday.
CHESTER	No.
SERGEANT	Right, then. Let's 'ave you!
CHESTER	But I've just moved in.
SERGEANT	This place was empty yesterday.
CHESTER	Well, it's not empty now, it's full! What do you think you're doing - barging into private property like this?
SERGEANT	There were two cars outside.
CHESTER	That's no reason to go bursting into other people's houses!
SERGEANT	Two cars that 'adn't been 'ere before. That's why I'm 'ere.
CHESTER	One belongs to me and one to my mother-in-law.
SERGEANT	(aghast) Don't tell me you're living with your mother-in-law?
CHESTER	I'm afraid so.
SERGEANT	Hard luck, mate.
CHESTER	What the hell's it got to do with you who I'm living with?

(The SERGEANT indicates his stripes.)

SERGEANT	See them? Not Scotch mist, you know.
CHESTER	But I'm not in the Army!
SERGEANT	You're in danger, though.
CHESTER	So are you.
SERGEANT	What's that?

CHESTER	If you don't leave at once I shall set my father-in-law on you.
SERGEANT	Now, look 'ere - I don't like your attitude!
CHESTER	That makes two of us! (He glares at him.)
SERGEANT	Don't you look at me like that.
CHESTER	I can't help how I look.
SERGEANT	I don't like it.
CHESTER	Well, you'll have to speak to my mother about that. (He moves away D.R.)
SERGEANT	Is _she_ 'ere, too?
CHESTER	No. She's in Littlehampton. Only don't go there because she wouldn't be in. Not today. It's her bridge afternoon.
SERGEANT	(moving to L. of CHESTER) Look - I'm from down the road!
CHESTER	I don't care where you're from - you're trespassing!
SERGEANT	You take my advice - pack up and get out!
CHESTER	But I haven't _unpacked_ yet.
SERGEANT	Good. Then you can get out even quicker.
CHESTER	This is my house and I live here!
SERGEANT	If you want to go _on_ living, you'd better get out.
CHESTER	What do you mean?
SERGEANT	Twenty-four hours and this place is going up.
CHESTER	Up?
SERGEANT	Bang!
CHESTER	What?
SERGEANT	Bang! Boom!
CHESTER	Going up bang-boom?
SERGEANT	Yes.
CHESTER	Why?
SERGEANT	Part of the exercise.

CHESTER	What exercise?
SERGEANT	Army exercise. You're in no-man's-land.
CHESTER	Am I?
SERGEANT	Yes.
CHESTER	I didn't know that.
SERGEANT	Right in the middle.
CHESTER	And that's not a good place to be?
SERGEANT	I wouldn't recommend it.
CHESTER	There must be some mistake.
SERGEANT	No mistake, mate. I should think there's enough dynamite in this place to destroy Buckingham Palace. You stay 'ere and this time tomorrow you'll be up there, singing 'Over the Rainbow'.
CHESTER	But I've only just bought this house!
SERGEANT	Freehold?
CHESTER	No. On a lease.
SERGEANT	That's what I thought. It expires tomorrow. (Moves to D.L.C., looking about.) I expect you got it cheap.
CHESTER	Well - yes - it was a little less than I expected.
SERGEANT	There you are, then. Buy a cheap house you can't expect it to last forever, can you?
CHESTER	Twenty-four hours?
SERGEANT	What?
CHESTER	That's not long for a lease.
SERGEANT	Long enough for you to get out.
	(CHESTER goes to the SERGEANT.)
CHESTER	(puzzled) The Estate Agent never mentioned dynamite.
SERGEANT	Well - he wouldn't, would he? Might have put you off the sale. You didn't ask, I suppose?
CHESTER	It never occurred to me!

SERGEANT	Oh, dear me. Bit reckless, eh? A bit of the old bravado.
CHESTER	If you're buying a house you don't expect it to explode the next day!
SERGEANT	You didn't get a surveyor in, then?
CHESTER	Well - no, I didn't.
SERGEANT	Pity. You'd have known then.
CHESTER	What do you mean?
SERGEANT	You'd have had it in writing - 'Woodworm, rising damp and dynamite'.
CHESTER	It's not likely to go off before tomorrow night, is it?
SERGEANT	Not unless you start firing guns in 'ere!
CHESTER	Well, that's more than likely! Whatever shall I tell my wife? I'm in enough trouble already. And her mother! She doesn't think much of the house as it is. God knows what she'll say if I tell her it's going to disappear tomorrow afternoon.
SERGEANT	I'll say one thing for you. You're one of the smartest squatters I've ever seen.
CHESTER	Squatters?
SERGEANT	That's what you're doing 'ere, isn't it? See a place empty for a while - boom-boom - in you go. Only this time it's going to be boom-boom out you go! (He laughs.)
CHESTER	I don't know what you're talking about.
SERGEANT	'Ere! You didn't really buy this place, did you?
CHESTER	Of course I bought it! It's mine!
SERGEANT	Oh, blimey! Somebody really took you for a ride, didn't they?
	(PATRICIA comes down the stairs to C. with an address book.)
PATRICIA	I've got the number. Will you 'phone her or shall I? (Sees the SERGEANT.) Oh, sorry.
CHESTER	Ah - yes - er - This is the Army. Well, not all of

	it, you understand.
SERGEANT	Sergeant Everest, Ma'am.
PATRICIA	How do you do.
CHESTER	The sergeant just popped in to warn us - er - to welcome us! Wasn't that nice of him?
PATRICIA	I'm afraid we're in a bit of a mess at the moment. We haven't really settled in yet.
SERGEANT	I'm very glad to 'ear it!
PATRICIA	What?
CHESTER	(going quickly to PATRICIA) Yes - well - you pop along, darling, and I'll see to the sergeant.
	(He passes her across to his L., urging her to go.)
PATRICIA	I'll 'phone her, then? I expect the number's in here.
CHESTER	What number?
PATRICIA	Your sister's number. The one with the suitcase.
CHESTER	Oh, no! No - I wouldn't! She's very funny on the 'phone. I'll do it.
PATRICIA	All right, then. You pop along and 'phone and I'll see to the sergeant.
CHESTER	No! That'd be worse.
PATRICIA	What?
CHESTER	Well, he's made his speech. He doesn't want to go through all that again. Do you? No. It was a very nice speech but once is enough.
	(MISS PARTRIDGE comes in from the kitchen, engrossed in her tour of discovery.)
MISS P	If these walls could speak they'd tell a thing or two!
CHESTER	Yes, I bet they would. What the hell's she doing here?
MISS P	This place is full of magic.
SERGEANT	It's full of something else as well.
	(MISS PARTRIDGE crosses below them to D. R., breathing the air of antiquity.)

MISS P	The rafters themselves are pregnant with a sense of the past! (She peers at the rafters.)
CHESTER	How did <u>she</u> get in?
PATRICIA	I don't know. She wasn't here when I went upstairs.
	(CAROL comes in from the kitchen. PATRICIA reacts.)
CAROL	It's all right. She hasn't taken the silver.
CHESTER	Silver? What are you talking about?
PATRICIA	You said she'd gone!
CHESTER	Who?
PATRICIA	Mrs Bounty!
CHESTER	Did I? Yes – well, she did the sprouts and came back. That was it, wasn't it?
	(CAROL sees the suitcase on the sofa table and goes to it.)
CAROL	What's my suitcase doing down here?
PATRICIA	<u>Your</u> suitcase?
CAROL	Yes.
	(PATRICIA turns coldly to CHESTER.)
PATRICIA	Perhaps your mother gave Mrs Bounty a suitcase as well?
CHESTER	Yes, she did! It was an offer in Littlehampton. Three for the price of two, and Mrs Bounty happened to be about so she got one. Wasn't that nice?
CAROL	And my dressing-gown!
	(CHESTER shrinks and laughs nervously.)
PATRICIA	(to CHESTER) I suppose <u>yours</u> is in blue?
	(A rattle of machine-gun fire from outside. Automatically CAROL runs into CHESTER's arms.)
MISS P	(ecstatic) There they go again!
	(CHESTER extricates himself quickly.)
CHESTER	What?

MISS P	Vibrations from the Middle Ages!
SERGEANT	What's she on about?
CHESTER	I've no idea. You wouldn't like to buy a house, would you?
SERGEANT	No fear!
	(ELROOD races on, carrying his shotgun. LADY ELROOD is following him.)
ELROOD	Get your heads down everybody!
PATRICIA	What's the matter?
ELROOD	Didn't you hear it? We're under fire! Take cover!
LADY E	Darling, there's nothing to get excited about.
ELROOD	I know gunfire when I hear it!
	(ELROOD sees the SERGEANT.)
	Good God! There's one of 'em inside!
	(He raises his gun threateningly and crosses above the sofa to the SERGEANT. The SERGEANT and CHESTER both fear for the dynamite.)
SERGEANT	No! Don't shoot! Please!
	(He backs away to D.C., ELROOD following.)
ELROOD	Get 'em up! Get 'em up!
SERGEANT	Now, sir - you put that thing down, eh?
ELROOD	Get 'em up!
CHESTER	Don't shoot! Not in here!
ELROOD	Three seconds and I fire!
SERGEANT	Oh, my God!
	The SERGEANT races through them all for the front door with ELROOD in pursuit. General chatter as they all call to ELROOD to be careful, etc. ABEL comes in from the kitchen in his raincoat in time to see ELROOD pursuing the SERGEANT out of the front door. There is a loud bang from outside as ELROOD fires. They all react and start running for the door as - THE CURTAIN FALLS

ACT TWO

Scene One

Early evening.

It is a pleasant sunny evening. The room has now
been tidied up a little, and there is a fire blazing in
the grate. A few potted plants here and there.

CAROL, still wearing CHESTER's shirt and trousers,
is kneeling down in front of the fire putting on some
logs. CHESTER comes downstairs urgently,
carrying a suitcase. He sees CAROL, and comes to
above the sofa.

CHESTER	There's no time for that!
CAROL	What?
CHESTER	Lighting fires and sitting down.
CAROL	Thought I'd make it nice and cosy.
CHESTER	(moving to her) You already have. Far too cosy.
CAROL	Isn't that what you wanted?
CHESTER	It was before I arrived, but now I'm here it's not. (He puts the suitcase down L. of the sofa.)
CAROL	Talk to him, then.
CHESTER	Who?
CAROL	Mr Bounty.
CHESTER	Is he still here? He said he was off.
CAROL	Your mother twisted his arm.
CHESTER	Who? Oh – my mother! The one here. (Moves to below the sofa.)
CAROL	She gave him a few words and that was that.
CHESTER	Yes, it would be.
CAROL	So he laid the fire and I'm keeping it going. We can have dinner in here.
CHESTER	There isn't any!

CAROL	I expect your sister brought something with her.
CHESTER	My sister?
CAROL	Patricia!
CHESTER	Oh - her! Yes.
CAROL	They're out in the kitchen waiting for Mr Bounty to pump up his primus.
CHESTER	Is that what he's doing? Good heavens. Well, at least that means we've got a few minutes before they come back.

(CAROL, misunderstanding him, looks pleased, rises and comes to him eagerly.)

CAROL	Yes, darling -
CHESTER	What?
CAROL	That's more like it.
CHESTER	More like what?
CAROL	The way you were in 'The Horse and Groom'. (She snuggles up to him.)
CHESTER	I'm sure I was never like this.
CAROL	Yes, you were. This and a lot more.
CHESTER	In the saloon bar?
CAROL	Well, come on! Be quick. They'll be back in a minute.
CHESTER	That's what I'm worried about. (He disengages himself and breaks away to D.C.)
CAROL	They won't mind.
CHESTER	That's what you think. (He turns to her.) Look, I've got to explain -
CAROL	The way you're carrying on anyone would think Patricia was your wife.
CHESTER	And the way you're carrying on anyone would think you were! Suppose they came in and found me in here with my arms around my own shirt?
CAROL	(going to him) Why should they object? They

	seemed awfully nice to me.
CHESTER	They may be awfully nice to you, but they wouldn't be awfully nice to me if I was awfully nice to you!
CAROL	I can't wait to tell them all about us!
CHESTER	There's nothing to tell!
CAROL	I'll tell them during dinner.
CHESTER	You mustn't do that!
CAROL	Why not? They must have seen you with a girl before.
CHESTER	Ah – yes – but you see – the thing is this. It's – it's Gladys.
CAROL	Who's Gladys?
CHESTER	Lives in Littlehampton. Round the corner from my mother.
CAROL	I don't know what you're talking about.
CHESTER	Oh, good.
CAROL	What's Gladys-round-the-corner-in-Littlehampton got to do with you putting your arms around me-with-your-shirt-on?
CHESTER	She's rather plain and plays the piano.
CAROL	Well?
CHESTER	No. Very badly. Both feet on the loud pedal.
CAROL	I mean – well, what about her?
CHESTER	Gladys?
CAROL	Yes.
CHESTER	My mother's very fond of her, you see, and so is my sister Patricia.
CAROL	In spite of the loud pedal?
CHESTER	Oh, she doesn't play all the time.
CAROL	The neighbours must be pleased.
CHESTER	And my mother and sister have always had this hope.
CAROL	That she'll stop playing the piano?

CHESTER	That she'll stop playing – no. No, that one day Gladys and I will marry.
CAROL	Other people?
CHESTER	Each other.
CAROL	Whatever for?
CHESTER	Well – you know – the usual reasons.
CAROL	You don't play the piano, do you?
CHESTER	No.
CAROL	Then it's out of the question. Put your arms around me. (She snuggles up to him again.)
CHESTER	(extricating himself) Look – it wouldn't do to be seen like this. They'd be very upset. Besides, if I know Gladys she'll be on her way here now. She'll probably arrive at any moment. And if she saw us like that – well, you can imagine.
	(A rattle of gunfire from down the road. She leaps back into his arms. ABEL comes in from the kitchen.)
ABEL	You two at it again?
CHESTER	We were taking cover. (He disengages himself.)
ABEL	She's going a treat now.
CHESTER	Is she?
ABEL	I pumped her up and that was that.
CHESTER	Oh – your primus!
ABEL	They want to know if corned beef hash is all right for dinner.
CAROL	There you are! I said your sister would have brought something with her.
ABEL	I haven't got a sister.
CAROL	Not yours, Abel. His.
ABEL	(to CHESTER) Don't tell me your sister's here as well?
CHESTER	Ah – yes – you didn't know that, did you? No. Well,

	she's here all right.
ABEL	Going to be a bit crowded in the bedrooms, isn't it? (See the suitcase CHESTER has brought down.) That's funny. I could have sworn I took that upstairs.
CHESTER	Yes – it's mine.
	(ABEL picks up the suitcase.)
ABEL	The proper place for this is up there, not down here.
CHESTER	(moving to below the sofa) Yes, Abel, I know. But the situation's changed, and now I want it down here.
ABEL	You mean you're not staying?
CHESTER	No.
CAROL	What?
CHESTER	Something's cropped up.
ABEL	So you're off then?
CHESTER	Soon.
CAROL	You never told me.
CHESTER	I didn't get the chance.
	(ABEL crosses to the window seat with CHESTER's suitcase.)
ABEL	There's another over there.
CHESTER	What?
ABEL	Suitcase. (He indicates CAROL's suitcase, which is near the window seat.)
CAROL	That's mine.
ABEL	(a glint in his eye) Aaah – I see. I'll put them together then, shall I? (He puts CHESTER's case with CAROL's.)
CHESTER	Anywhere you like, Abel.
ABEL	Then they'll be handy, sir, won't they? (He chuckles.)
CAROL	What's the matter with him?

CHESTER	I expect he's been pumping his primus too much.
ABEL	Don't worry. I won't say a word. (He goes towards the kitchen.)
CHESTER	What about?
ABEL	About you two going off together.
CHESTER	What?!
CAROL	(hopefully) Are we?
ABEL	You'll have some corned beef hash first, though. (He goes off into the kitchen.)
	(CAROL immediately embraces CHESTER delightedly.)
CAROL	You never told me we were leaving.
CHESTER	Well, I didn't know, did I?
CAROL	When did you decide?
CHESTER	Oh - a little while ago Something unexpected cropped up.
CAROL	And you never said anything.
CHESTER	No. And I've got to tell everyone, but I don't know how to put it.
CAROL	We can't tell them!
CHESTER	Why not?
CAROL	Don't be silly. What about Gladys?
CHESTER	This doesn't concern Gladys. She's not here, is she?
CAROL	(delighted) Oh, darling! (She embraces him.)
CHESTER	(extricating himself and moving away R. C.) You really must stop doing that.
CAROL	All right. There'll be plenty of time later on.
CHESTER	Will there?
CAROL	But I really don't think you should tell them.
CHESTER	We can't leave them here!
CAROL	Why not?
CHESTER	Because if we do, this time tomorrow they'll be up

there singing 'Over the Rainbow'.

CAROL	(crossing to him) What are you talking about?
CHESTER	If I told you, you'd never believe me. That's the trouble - nobody will. But one thing's certain - we can't stay here!
CAROL	Good. Then I'd better take your clothes off.
CHESTER	What?
CAROL	These! (Indicates the clothes she has on.)
CHESTER	Oh.
CAROL	My dress should be dry by now. (She goes towards the stairs.) I shan't be long. Isn't this exciting? (She goes off upstairs, happily.)

(CHESTER is left, bemused and bewildered. He takes up the whisky and starts to pour himself a drink, looking R. MISS PARTRIDGE comes in from the kitchen. She is studying an old map intently and does not at first see CHESTER, nor he her as he is busy pouring out his drink. Therefore they collide and both jump.)

CHESTER	Aah! (He sees her and immediately takes a large drink of whisky.)
MISS P	I expect you can feel it, can't you?
CHESTER	Yes, I can. Very warming. I think I'll have some more. (He takes another sip.)
MISS P	I beg your pardon?
CHESTER	The whisky. Very warming.
MISS P	No, no. The atmosphere of antiquity!
CHESTER	Oh, that. Yes, it is a bit damp, isn't it?
MISS P	There's a spot over here where, if you stand very still and close your eyes, you can almost believe you're back in the Middle Ages.
CHESTER	Really?
MISS P	Oh, yes. Would you like to try?
CHESTER	Not a lot.

MISS P	For me.
CHESTER	Oh, all right. Is it far?
MISS P	Just over here. (She goes to a spot near the window seat.)
CHESTER	You don't mind if I bring the bottle with me?
MISS P	H'm?
CHESTER	Never mind.
MISS P	It's just here.
CHESTER	Right. (He joins her.) This the spot?
MISS P	Yes. Now - take my hand.
CHESTER	What?
MISS P	Take my hand. Together the influence will be twice as strong.
CHESTER	Will it?
MISS P	Oh, yes.
CHESTER	Right.
	(They hold hands.)
MISS P	Now - close your eyes.
	(He closes his eyes and opens them again quickly.)
CHESTER	You as well!
MISS P	Of course.
CHESTER	No cheating, mind.
MISS P	Ready?
CHESTER	Now?
MISS P	Yes.
CHESTER	Right.
	(They close their eyes.)
MISS P	Closed?
CHESTER	Yes.
MISS P	Now - breathe in deeply.

CHESTER	Right.
	(Together they slowly breathe in deeply and slowly out again.)
MISS P	Did you get anything?
CHESTER	Corned beef hash.
MISS P	Try again.
CHESTER	Right.
	(Together, holding hands, their eyes closed, they breathe in deeply a few times. LADY ELROOD comes in from the kitchen and stops as she sees them. They continue, oblivious of her presence. Eventually -)
LADY E	Whatever's going on?
	(They open their eyes. CHESTER feels ridiculous and breaks away to R. of the sofa.)
	What were you doing?
CHESTER	We were reaching for the Reformation.
MISS P	It was there!
CHESTER	Was it?
LADY E	What was there?
MISS P	The atmosphere of antiquity. I've been studying maps and dates, and this house must have been right in the path of Cromwell. I'm surprised it wasn't razed to the ground.
CHESTER	It soon will be.
	(LADY ELROOD moves to below the sofa.)
LADY E	What did you say?
CHESTER	I said I expect it soon will be. You know what it's like these days - new roads everywhere, pulling everything down.
LADY E	I presume you made the necessary searches?
CHESTER	Oh, yes. There's nothing but old cans of paint out there.

LADY E	Not those sort of searches! Legal formalities!
CHESTER	Well, there wasn't a lot of time.
MISS P	Partridge.
LADY E	I beg your pardon?
MISS P	That's my name. Miss Partridge.
LADY E	Yes, well, I can't imagine what you're doing here, Miss Partridge.
MISS P	I was drawn here inexorably! This place is full of history and you can't keep me away from that.
LADY E	(gently) Miss Partridge - this is a private house. People are living here.
MISS P	They said in the village it had been empty for ages.
LADY E	Yes, it was. They were waiting for some idiot to come and buy it.
CHESTER	And then I came along.
LADY E	Exactly!
CHESTER	What?
LADY E	(to MISS P) So it was empty, but now it's full.
MISS P	That's quite all right. You won't be in my way.
LADY E	There isn't enough corned beef hash to go around.
CHESTER	Thank goodness for that.
LADY E	(firmly) There's some for you!
CHESTER	What a pity.
MISS P	You needn't worry about me. I brought my sandwiches and a thermos of beef tea.
CHESTER	Oh, good!
MISS P	There's a cellar here.
LADY E	You don't have to sit in the cellar, Miss Partridge. You can have your sandwiches here by the fire.
MISS P	Oh - thank you. (To CHESTER.) Have you been there?

CHESTER	Where?
MISS P	The cellar.
CHESTER	I didn't know there was one.
MISS P	Well, it's on my plan.
CHESTER	Of course! That'll be where he's put it.
LADY E	Put what?
CHESTER	No wonder I couldn't find it anywhere.
LADY E	What are you talking about?
CHESTER	Oh - er - the gas meter! The man will want to see it. Won't he? Read it. Yes.
MISS P	I should think it's steeped in spirits of the past.
CHESTER	Well, I wish it was steeped in spirits of the present. This isn't going to last much longer. (He glances at the rapidly diminishing whisky in the bottle.)
MISS P	I think I'll explore through here. (She heads for the door D. R.) Sure you won't join me?
CHESTER	No. Not just now. (To LADY E.) How about you, Mummy?
LADY E	Not for me!
CHESTER	Not for her. You won't go into the cellar, will you?
MISS P	(vaguely) I beg your pardon?
CHESTER	We don't want you striking matches down there.
LADY E	Is there a leak?
CHESTER	I wish that was all!
MISS P	Don't forget - deep breaths!
CHESTER	I'll remember.
	(She goes, elated, D. R.)
LADY E	(moving to L. of CHESTER) Who on earth let her in?
CHESTER	I expect she just walked in. Like everybody else.
LADY E	I came here to work!

	(A roll of gunfire. Without thinking, CHESTER grabs LADY ELROOD. She pulls away at once.)
	Don't start that with me!
CHESTER	I thought you were someone else.
LADY E	Mrs Bounty, no doubt?
CHESTER	What?
LADY E	Don't think I've forgotten what I saw.
CHESTER	No, I'm sure you haven't.
LADY E	She's gone home, I take it?
CHESTER	No. She's gone upstairs to put her clothes on.
LADY E	What?!
CHESTER	I mean – to take them off! No – I mean – to take mine off and put hers on.
LADY E	Poor Mr Bounty. I can't imagine why he ever married a girl like that.
CHESTER	Oh, I can –
	(As LADY ELROOD glares at him.)
	She's very good at sprouts.
	(PATRICIA comes out of the kitchen.)
PATRICIA	Darling, will those guns be going on all night?
CHESTER	(crossing to her delightedly, seeing an escape) Yes! Rather! I'm afraid they will. All night!
LADY E	Nonsense! Even soldiers must sleep. (She goes towards the window seat.)
CHESTER	This is the night shift.
PATRICIA	Oh, dear. (Resigned.) Well, I suppose we'll just have to put up with it.
CHESTER	No, you won't!
PATRICIA	Don't be silly, darling. They're not going to stop shooting because we don't like the noise.
LADY E	I can't think how you came to buy a house with gunfire in the first place.

PATRICIA	I suppose we'll just have to be content with peaceful Sundays.
CHESTER	There won't be any of those!
PATRICIA	But you said –
CHESTER	I know I did. But it wasn't true. That's what the sergeant came to tell me. They're having manoeuvres on Sundays from now on. They'll be sprawling all over the place, shouting and shooting all through the Sabbath.
PATRICIA	(with a shrug) I expect we'll get used to it.
CHESTER	Of course you won't!
PATRICIA	What?
CHESTER	You'll never get used to it!
PATRICIA	Honestly – I don't mind.
CHESTER	Of course you mind.
PATRICIA	I don't!
CHESTER	Well, you should mind! I mind! She minds. (To LADY E.) Don't you? Yes. She minds a lot.
LADY E	I shan't be living here.
CHESTER	Neither will I.
PATRICIA	I don't understand you. I thought you liked the house and you wanted me to like it.
CHESTER	Yes, I did. But that was before and this is after. I've gone off it now. It's a good thing we didn't unpack.
PATRICIA	But we did.
CHESTER	Ah, yes – but now I've packed again. Packed it up and brought it down and there it is.
PATRICIA	What?
CHESTER	My suitcase. Over there.
LADY E	I shall go to 'The Horse and Groom'.
CHESTER	They'll be glad of that.

(Urging PATRICIA round L. of the sofa towards the stairs.)

So you go and do yours and then we can all pop off.

(PATRICIA stops him.)

PATRICIA   Chester, do be sensible. You've bought this place. It's ours. We can't move in and then move straight out again.

CHESTER   Why not? I've had enough of it.

PATRICIA   We've only been here three hours! We haven't given it a chance.

CHESTER   Darling, I'll find you another house. A much nicer house with no gunfire in the garden.

PATRICIA   (getting fed up with him)   But I like this house! (She moves away to below the sofa.)

CHESTER   How can you possibly like it? Look at it!

PATRICIA   It's beautiful!

LADY E   (calmly)   Why don't we all sit down quietly, have our corned beef hash and talk it over?

                  (PATRICIA sinks onto the sofa.)

PATRICIA   (starting to cry, deliberately)   This is my first house and I'm not going to leave it -

CHESTER   Oh, my God -

LADY E   Why don't you give it two or three days and see how you feel?

CHESTER   Two or three days? That'll be far too late.

LADY E   Too late?

CHESTER   Yes. This time tomorrow we shall be up there singing 'Over the Rainbow'!

                  (They do not know what the hell he is talking about. CAROL comes downstairs. She is now wearing her dress, which is short, tight-fitting and low-cut. She comes to U.C.)

CAROL   Well - I'm ready!

                  (They all react.)

	My dress <u>had</u> dried out all right.
CHESTER	Looks as if it's shrunk a bit, too.
CAROL	Oh, no. This is how it was made.
CHESTER	Good heavens –
	(CAROL sees PATRICIA sniffling into her handker-chief and wrongly assumes that she is upset over Gladys.)
CAROL	Oh, dear. You've told them, then?
CHESTER	Told them?
CAROL	About <u>us</u> going away together.
	(PATRICIA and LADY ELROOD react. CHESTER wishes he was elsewhere.)
PATRICIA	(grimly) I see. Well, I might have known! (She rises and goes angrily towards the stairs.)
CHESTER	Just a minute! I can explain –
PATRICIA	Yes, I bet you can!
CHESTER	Where are you going?
PATRICIA	To borrow my father's shotgun! (She goes off, angrily.)
	(CHESTER goes to CAROL.)
CHESTER	Now see what you've done. I'm going to be shot in my own house. (To LADY ELROOD.) She misunderstood.
LADY E	A likely tale!
CAROL	(to LADY E) You mustn't worry.
LADY E	Thank you very much.
CAROL	I promise you, it'll be all right. I'll explain it all to Gladys.
LADY E	Gladys? Have you gone mad?
CAROL	What?
LADY E	I shall go and commiserate with Mr Bounty. (She goes off to the kitchen.)

CAROL	Hadn't you told them?
CHESTER	No, of course I hadn't!
CAROL	I didn't expect them to react quite so strongly. They must be awfully fond of Gladys.
CHESTER	Yes. I told you. They are. Especially my sister. I'd better go and speak to her.
	(He goes towards the stairs. She follows him.)
CAROL	Be careful!
CHESTER	Don't worry. I'm used to getting out of the way of that shotgun. (He goes off upstairs.)
	(The front door opens and MRS BOUNTY comes in. She is in her late 40s, a timid woman in a hat.)
MRS BOUNTY	Is he still here?
CAROL	I beg your pardon?
MRS BOUNTY	He hasn't gone yet, then? I thought I might be too late.
	(CAROL makes another wrong assumption and crosses to MRS BOUNTY.)
CAROL	Oh, no. He's still here. He's just gone upstairs. As a matter of fact, he said you might arrive at any moment.
MRS BOUNTY	(puzzled) He did?
CAROL	Oh, yes. You knew he was going, then?
MRS BOUNTY	Well, he couldn't stay for ever, could he?
CAROL	No. I suppose not.
MRS BOUNTY	Might have known he'd hang around here with you dressed like that, though. Good thing I turned up, by the look of it. He'd be hard pressed to keep his mind on his work, I reckon.
CAROL	Oh, I haven't had this dress on all the time.
MRS BOUNTY	(suspiciously) Oh, no?
CAROL	I've just put it back on. He was very kind and lent me his shirt and trousers.

MRS BOUNTY	Sounds to me as if he's been up to no good. (She goes below CAROL to D.C.)
CAROL	He talked about you a lot.
MRS BOUNTY	Oh, yes?
CAROL	(moving to R. of MRS BOUNTY) Have you just arrived, then?
MRS BOUNTY	'Course I have.
CAROL	By train?
MRS BOUNTY	(puzzled) Train? Came on my bike, didn't I?
CAROL	Bike?
MRS BOUNTY	That's right.
CAROL	All the way?
MRS BOUNTY	Well - I walked the last few yards.
CAROL	It's such a long way from Littlehampton!

(MRS BOUNTY, naturally, cannot think what she is talking about.)

MRS BOUNTY	Is it?
CAROL	Oh, yes. (Pause.) Especially on a bicycle.
MRS BOUNTY	(thoughtfully) Depends where you're going, I suppose.
CAROL	He says you play the piano very beautifully.
MRS BOUNTY	Does he?
CAROL	Would you like a bit of advice?
MRS BOUNTY	If you like.

(CAROL comes closer to impart great wisdom.)

CAROL	Keep your foot off the loud pedal.
MRS BOUNTY	Eh?
CAROL	It'll make all the difference.
MRS BOUNTY	I'll try to remember. (She heads for the stairs.) Upstairs, you said?
CAROL	Just a minute!

(MRS BOUNTY stops.)

There's something you ought to know.

MRS BOUNTY   Oh, yes?

CAROL   You'd be bound to find out one day, so I may as well tell you now.

MRS BOUNTY   I dunno what you're talking about.

CAROL   You've got to be awfully brave.

MRS BOUNTY   Have I?

CAROL   It'll be a terrible shock at first, but you must try hard not to hate him. If you really love him and want him to be happy you'll concentrate on your piano - make beautiful music in Littlehampton - and everything will be all right.

MRS BOUNTY   Don't think I fancy Littlehampton -

CAROL   That's what you think now, but believe me you'll grow to love it!

MRS BOUNTY   I went to Frinton last year. That was all right. Not so sure about Littlehampton, though.

CAROL   I think you'd better sit down.

(She leads the bewildered MRS BOUNTY to the sofa and sits her down.)

Would you like some whisky? I think there's some left.

MRS BOUNTY   I thought you must have been drinking!

CAROL   I've only had one.

MRS BOUNTY   I don't think I'll bother, thank you.

CAROL   Well - all right - but it's there if you want it. (She sits beside her.)   Are you ready?

MRS BOUNTY   I reckon so.

CAROL   It all happened in 'The Horse and Groom'.

MRS BOUNTY   That doesn't surprise me. He spends far too much time in there.

CAROL   We got talking. You know how it is.

MRS BOUNTY   He doesn't usually take his nose out of the glass.
                  Did you have your dress on at the time?

CAROL   What? Oh, yes.

MRS BOUNTY   Can't understand it, then.

CAROL   Anyhow, that's where it all began.

MRS BOUNTY   I see.

CAROL   Something happened to us in the saloon bar –

MRS BOUNTY   Saloon, eh?

CAROL   And now there's nothing anybody can do to stop us.
                  We're going away together!

                  (CAROL waits with bated breath for the explosion of
                  outrage. MRS BOUNTY looks at her calmly.)

MRS BOUNTY   You and him?

CAROL   Yes.

                  (MRS BOUNTY considers this for a moment.)

MRS BOUNTY   To Littlehampton?

CAROL   Oh, no! We couldn't go there.

MRS BOUNTY   No. I don't blame you.   (Pause.)   You'd like
                  Frinton better than Littlehampton.

CAROL   (a little put out)   Does it matter where we're going?

MRS BOUNTY   Should have thought it mattered to you. You sure
                  you've made up your mind?

CAROL   You don't seem very upset.

MRS BOUNTY   More surprised, I'd say. I'd have thought you'd
                  want someone a bit more lively.

CAROL   You've obviously never seen him at his best.

MRS BOUNTY   Apparently not. I'll have to take another look at him,
                  I reckon.

CAROL   I'm so glad you're not angry. I can see it's going to be
                  all right. I'll go and tell him at once!   (She goes
                  joyfully upstairs.)

                  (MRS BOUNTY is left wondering. She sees the

whisky, reaches for it and is about to open it when
there is a gunshot from outside. She freezes.
LORD ELROOD races in, his shotgun under his arm.
He sees MRS BOUNTY and comes to C.)

ELROOD	There's a lot of movement on the ground out there.
MRS BOUNTY	Them's rabbits, I expect.
ELROOD	I beg your pardon?
MRS BOUNTY	That what you're after? Rabbits?
ELROOD	Don't waste valuable ammunition on rabbits, you know.
MRS BOUNTY	You won't find much else worth shooting around here.
ELROOD	Don't you be too sure.
MRS BOUNTY	A few ducks, maybe.
ELROOD	Wouldn't be surprised to see them closing in soon. Try to surround us as soon as it's dark.
MRS BOUNTY	The ducks?
ELROOD	The enemy!
MRS BOUNTY	Didn't know there was one.

(He comes to her.)

ELROOD	Haven't seen you before.
MRS BOUNTY	I came here to help this morning.
ELROOD	Ah! Reinforcements! Why didn't you say so? Excellent! Well, don't stand about here. There's plenty to be done. (Makes for the stairs.) If anybody wants me, tell 'em I've gone to change the guard! (He goes off upstairs.)

(MRS BOUNTY looks bewildered. She takes a quick
drink. ABEL comes in from the kitchen. She looks
at him with new eyes. He is surprised to see her
there.)

ABEL	Didn't know you was coming back.
MRS BOUNTY	Good thing I did by the sound of it.
ABEL	Eh?

MRS BOUNTY	Turn you around.
ABEL	What for?
MRS BOUNTY	Turn you around. I want to have a good look at you.
ABEL	What you talking about?
MRS BOUNTY	Just do as I say.
	(Reluctantly, and feeling rather ridiculous, ABEL ' turns slowly around. She watches him carefully.)
ABEL	All right?
MRS BOUNTY	Still look the same to me.
ABEL	Why should I look any different?
MRS BOUNTY	From what I've heard I thought perhaps you'd turned into a sex symbol or something.
ABEL	I've been pumping up my primus.
MRS BOUNTY	That's not all you've been doing from what I hear!
ABEL	I'm getting a man to see to it in the morning.
MRS BOUNTY	See to what?
ABEL	The gas cooker! It's gone wonky. That's why I had to fall back on my primus.
MRS BOUNTY	Was that before you took your trousers off?
ABEL	You been drinking?
MRS BOUNTY	Not for long.
ABEL	Took my trousers off?
MRS BOUNTY	Fine sight you must have been. Especially today.
ABEL	What's special today?
MRS BOUNTY	You've got your purple pants on.
ABEL	Why should I take my trousers off in the middle of the afternoon?
MRS BOUNTY	Well, I suppose she'd taken her dress off so you felt a bit out of it.
ABEL	(realising) Ah! Now I know who you're talking about!

MRS BOUNTY	You remember her taking her dress off, then?
ABEL	'Course I remember! But that wasn't down here. That was upstairs.
MRS BOUNTY	You ought to be ashamed of yourself! Chasing after young girls at your time of life. I suppose Little-hampton was <u>your</u> idea?
ABEL	Eh?
MRS BOUNTY	If you had to take her anywhere why couldn't you pick somewhere like Frinton? Nice sands at Frinton.
ABEL	I'm not taking her anywhere! She came here to find Mr Dreadnought.
MRS BOUNTY	She said you lent her your trousers.
ABEL	That was him, not me. Standing here talking to you, I'm forgetting what I was about.
MRS BOUNTY	And what was that?
ABEL	More paraffin for the primus. It's out in the shed. (He makes for the front door.)
MRS BOUNTY	So it's him she's going off with?
ABEL	Yes. Them's their cases over there.
MRS BOUNTY	I might have known it wasn't you.
ABEL	Not so much of that! Could have been me, all right, if I'd put me mind to it. Purple pants or no purple pants! (He goes out.)
	(CAROL comes downstairs with PATRICIA, who is carrying the shotgun.)
CAROL	You don't <u>have</u> to believe me! Just come and ask her yourself.
PATRICIA	I don't know what you're talking about.
CAROL	Well, you'll soon see.
	(They come to C. and face MRS BOUNTY. CAROL indicates her triumphantly.)
	There you are!
	(PATRICIA looks puzzled, faced with a completely

	strange woman.)
PATRICIA	What?
CAROL	There she is!
	(PATRICIA looks at MRS BOUNTY, smiles weakly and looks back to CAROL.)
PATRICIA	Who?
CAROL	Gladys, of course.
	(PATRICIA and MRS BOUNTY look equally puzzled.)
	She's come all the way from Littlehampton on her bicycle.
PATRICIA	Good heavens -
	(PATRICIA and MRS BOUNTY remain impassive, having no idea what CAROL is talking about.)
CAROL	Well - go on, then. Ask her!
	(PATRICIA crosses below CAROL to R. of the sofa.)
PATRICIA	(to MRS BOUNTY) Did you have a good journey?
CAROL	No, not that!
MRS BOUNTY	(vaguely) Well, I got here, didn't I?
	(A pause.)
PATRICIA	You must have very strong legs.
MRS BOUNTY	What?
PATRICIA	All that pedalling.
MRS BOUNTY	Oh. Yes.
	(They fall into silence again.)
PATRICIA	There'll be corned beef hash in a minute. I expect you're very hungry.
MRS BOUNTY	Oh, don't you worry about me.
	(Another silence. CAROL waits patiently for PATRICIA to come to the point, and smiles encouragingly.)
PATRICIA	Do you do this sort of thing a lot?

MRS BOUNTY	Do what?
PATRICIA	Long distance bicycling.
	(MRS BOUNTY. smiles good-humouredly. She indicates the gun that PATRICIA is carrying.)
MRS BOUNTY	You going to try and shoot a rabbit?
PATRICIA	Not a rabbit, no!
CAROL	She was so angry with Chester that she chased him with the shotgun.
PATRICIA	He was too quick for me, though. He's locked himself in the lavatory.
MRS BOUNTY	You might have killed him!
PATRICIA	That was the idea.
CAROL	And all because of you!
MRS BOUNTY	Me?
CAROL	She didn't want you to be unhappy.
MRS BOUNTY	I wish you'd tell me what you're talking about.
CAROL	It's lucky you came, or heaven knows what would have happened. (To PATRICIA.) All right – now you can ask Gladys for yourself and then you won't have to worry about her any more.
PATRICIA	Gladys – ?
	(CAROL goes round the sofa to L. of MRS BOUNTY.)
CAROL	(to MRS BOUNTY) Go on – you tell her.
MRS BOUNTY	Eh?
CAROL	That you're not angry. That you don't mind. That you're going to go back to Littlehampton and play beautiful music!
MRS BOUNTY	But what have I got to be angry about?
CAROL	About Chester going off!
MRS BOUNTY	Why should I be angry about that?
CAROL	(to PATRICIA) You see! She doesn't mind.
MRS BOUNTY	He can do what he likes as far as I'm concerned.

But what's it got to do with <u>her</u>, anyhow?
(Pointing at PATRICIA.)

CAROL   She didn't want him to upset you.

MRS BOUNTY   It don't make no difference to me.

CAROL   (to PATRICIA)   There! You see?   (To MRS
                BOUNTY.)   So you aren't angry and you don't mind?

MRS BOUNTY   That's right.

CAROL   Oh, good!

                (She sits on the sofa and embraces the astonished
                MRS BOUNTY.)

MRS BOUNTY   But I'm not so sure about going to Littlehampton.

CAROL   Too many memories, you mean?

MRS BOUNTY   Well –

CAROL   Never mind. You can settle somewhere else.
                Anywhere you like. After all – the only thing you
                really need is a piano.

                (ABEL comes in from the front door with a can of
                paraffin.)

ABEL   I reckon this'll keep us going until the man comes in
                the morning.   (He sees PATRICIA with the shot-
                gun.)   You got it away from him all right, then?

PATRICIA   What?

ABEL   I should put it down if I were you, miss. Them
                things have a nasty way of going off.

                (CAROL rises and goes to take it from her.)

CAROL   I'll put it down over here, shall I?   (She takes it to
                the window seat R.)

ABEL   You see, miss – he might have left it loaded.

PATRICIA   I hope he has!

CAROL   But everything's all right now, isn't it? Thanks to
                Gladys. You won't need to use this after all.

PATRICIA   I wouldn't be too sure about that.

                (CAROL takes ABEL across to MRS BOUNTY.)

CAROL	Now, Abel – you come over here. Gladys – this is Abel.
ABEL	Gladys?
CAROL	Abel Bounty.
MRS BOUNTY	Yes. I <u>have</u> seen him before.
CAROL	You have? Oh, good. (To ABEL.) She's had a very long trip and she must be tired out.
ABEL	She didn't walk here, you know. She had her bike with her.
CAROL	It's a long way to Littlehampton!
	(ABEL looks at MRS BOUNTY. She shrugs.)
ABEL	I'd better go and see to my primus. (He goes towards the kitchen.)
CAROL	There'll be enough corned beef hash for one more, won't there, Abel?
ABEL	I dare say.
CAROL	That's all right, then.
ABEL	You expecting another one, then?
CAROL	No, but I'm sure Gladys would like some before she starts her journey home.
ABEL	I see – (He goes off to the kitchen with his can of paraffin.)
MRS BOUNTY	It's very kind of you, but I'll have something when I get home.
CAROL	Good heavens, you can't wait all that time. It'll be ready in a few minutes. Now – you come with me.
	(She leads her towards the stairs.)
MRS BOUNTY	Where we going?
CAROL	To see Chester. After all, <u>he</u> doesn't know you're here yet.
MRS BOUNTY	You said he was locked in the lavatory.
CAROL	He'll soon come out when he knows <u>you're</u> here!

(They go off upstairs, leaving PATRICIA completely
at sea. MISS PARTRIDGE comes in from the cellar.)

MISS P   You wouldn't believe what I've found down there.

PATRICIA   And you wouldn't believe what I've found up here!

MISS P   I feel that with every step I may be treading on Roman
              remains.

PATRICIA   You'll have to be more careful, then, won't you?

              (MISS PARTRIDGE produces an old pottery vase from
              her bag and thrusts it at PATRICIA.)

MISS P   Look at that!

PATRICIA   What is it?

MISS P   Medieval pottery.

PATRICIA   Are you sure?

MISS P   Oh, yes. It's positively pulsating with the past!

PATRICIA   I'd never have known.

MISS P   That's because you aren't in tune with history. I only
              have to close my eyes and touch it and my whole
              body throbs with anticipation!

PATRICIA   How very nice for you.

              (MISS PARTRIDGE puts the vase down on the table R.
              of the sofa.)

MISS P   Do you know what else I found in the cellar?

PATRICIA   (uninterested)   I haven't the faintest idea.

MISS P   Lots of little sticks in boxes. At first I thought it was
              dynamite. But it couldn't be, could it?

PATRICIA   (long-suffering)   No, Miss Partridge. I don't think
              so.

MISS P   Some sort of medieval candles, I suppose.
              (She delves into her bag and brings out a thermos
              flask.)

PATRICIA   (helpfully)   Another relic?

MISS P   Oh, no. My dinner.

PATRICIA	I'm so sorry.
MISS P	I won't be any trouble. (She goes to the sofa.)
PATRICIA	Please make yourself comfortable.
MISS P	Thank you.
	(She sits on the sofa. During the next scene she quietly gets on with her picnic. CHESTER comes in from the front door. He is a little breathless, his hair untidy. He does not see PATRICIA at first. She watches him as he brushes down his clothes with his hands. Eventually -)
PATRICIA	Well?
	(He jumps.)
CHESTER	Ah!
PATRICIA	Where have you been?
CHESTER	Er - looking for you!
PATRICIA	Out there?
CHESTER	Yes.
PATRICIA	But I was in here.
CHESTER	Yes. I can see that now. You were in here and I was out there.
PATRICIA	But how did you get out there?
CHESTER	What?
PATRICIA	You were upstairs. Locked in the -
CHESTER	Yes. I know.
PATRICIA	So how did you get out there?
CHESTER	There's a tree outside the window. I climbed.
PATRICIA	You didn't have to do that.
CHESTER	No. I could have opened the door, couldn't I?
PATRICIA	Yes.
CHESTER	And had my head blown off!
PATRICIA	There's still time!

CHESTER   Is there?

(She moves quickly for the gun. He sees what she is after and follows quickly.)

Oh, no!

(He struggles with her for the gun.)

Give me that!

PATRICIA   I'm going to kill you!

CHESTER   You can't do that.

PATRICIA   Why not?

CHESTER   There's somebody sitting on the sofa.

PATRICIA   It's only Miss Partridge!

(MISS PARTRIDGE looks up.)

MISS P   Yes, dear?

PATRICIA   I was just telling him it was only you.

MISS P   Oh, I see.

CHESTER   Hullo, Miss Partridge!

MISS P   Are you all right, dear?

PATRICIA   Yes, thank you.

MISS P   Oh, good.   (She goes back to her beef tea.)

CHESTER   Look - I can explain!

PATRICIA   Not any more! I'm going to kill you!

CHESTER   In front of Miss Partridge?

MISS P   Would you like a cup of beef tea?

CHESTER   Er - well - no, thanks. Not for me.   (To PATRICIA.)   Would you - er - ?

PATRICIA   No!

CHESTER   There's no need to shout. She only asked. No, thank you, Miss Partridge. Very kind of you to offer.

MISS P   There's plenty here if you change your mind.
(Busies herself with her sandwiches.)

CHESTER	Oh, good.
PATRICIA	Now I know why Mrs Bounty took her clothes off.
CHESTER	Please. Not in front of the Partridge.
PATRICIA	You needn't worry about her. She's too wrapped up in the past to hear anything.
CHESTER	She didn't take her clothes off. It was only her dress. It got wet in the rain. And it all happened before I arrived, anyway.
PATRICIA	So when you arrived she'd got her dress off all ready?
CHESTER	She was in her dressing-gown!
PATRICIA	Why did she have her dressing-gown with her?
CHESTER	I don't know!
MISS P	Would you like a sandwich?
CHESTER	What?
MISS P	Marmite or honey.
CHESTER	(to PATRICIA) Marmite or honey?
PATRICIA	No, thank you!
CHESTER	(to MISS PARTRIDGE) No, thank you.
PATRICIA	Presumably for the same reason she brought her suitcase – so that she was ready to go away with you!
CHESTER	I didn't even know she was going to be here.
	(LORD ELROOD comes to the top of the stairs.)
ELROOD	Ah! So you've got it!
PATRICIA	What?
ELROOD	My shotgun!
PATRICIA	I only borrowed it.
	(He comes down the stairs to them.)
ELROOD	Turned my back for two minutes and it was gone. Thought at first one of the enemy must have crept up on me.

PATRICIA	No. It was me.
CHESTER	Not asleep at your post, surely?
ELROOD	Good God, no! They'd be lucky to catch me napping.
CHESTER	Well, she did.
ELROOD	Yes. Well – less said about that to the men the better. (Sees MISS PARTRIDGE.) Whatever's that?
PATRICIA	Where?
ELROOD	On the sofa.
PATRICIA	Oh, that's Miss Partridge.
ELROOD	She one of ours?
PATRICIA	Yes.
MISS P	Would you like a sandwich?
ELROOD	No, thanks. Better get back to my post. (He starts to go.)
CHESTER	Aren't you forgetting something?
ELROOD	H'm? Oh, yes. (He comes back and takes the gun.) Hit anything?
PATRICIA	Unfortunately not.
ELROOD	You need more practice.
	(A rattle of gunfire outside.)
	Oh, my God! You see what happens when I leave my left flank exposed! (He rushes off.)
CHESTER	Darling –
PATRICIA	Don't you call me that!
CHESTER	Mrs Bounty would never go off with me. I'm employing her husband.
PATRICIA	He's a lot older than she is.
CHESTER	What's that got to do with it?
PATRICIA	She might easily go off with a younger man – no matter what he was like.

CHESTER	Thanks very much. (Moves away to R. of the sofa.)
PATRICIA	Look - there are both your cases - side by side - his and hers - all ready for the off! If you weren't anywhere, why did you pack your bag again?
CHESTER	Ah - yes - well, I am going.
PATRICIA	What?
CHESTER	But not with her.
PATRICIA	You expect me to believe that? (Moves away to the window seat.)
CHESTER	No. I shouldn't think there's much hope.
PATRICIA	(turning back) She even said you were going!
CHESTER	She misunderstood.
PATRICIA	And apparently everything's all right because that woman says she doesn't mind!
CHESTER	Mrs Bounty?
PATRICIA	No, not her. The other woman.
	(CHESTER goes halfway to her.)
CHESTER	What other woman?
PATRICIA	The other woman who was here.
CHESTER	(indicating MISS PARTRIDGE) Not - ?
PATRICIA	No!
CHESTER	Then what woman?
PATRICIA	The one who arrived.
CHESTER	When?
PATRICIA	Just now.
CHESTER	And she said it was all right for me to go off with Mrs Bounty?
PATRICIA	Yes.
CHESTER	What's it got to do with her?
PATRICIA	I don't know!

MISS P	I've got one Marmite sandwich left.　Would anybody like it?
CHESTER	H'm?　Oh, no, thanks.　　　(To PATRICIA.)　　You don't want a Marmite sandwich, do you?　No, I didn't think you would.　And she just came in and said it was all right?
PATRICIA	Yes.
CHESTER	What a nerve!　Where is she now?
PATRICIA	Gone upstairs.
CHESTER	She's not going to take her dress off, is she?
PATRICIA	Well, she's gone to look for you.　Whether that's a preliminary to taking her dress off, I don't know. Anyway, Mrs Bounty seemed to think you'd be pleased to see this woman.
CHESTER	Really?
PATRICIA	That's why they went to find you.
	(He moves U. S. , looking towards the stairs.)
CHESTER	(with a chuckle)　　　They're probably still banging on the lavatory door!　Why should I be pleased?
PATRICIA	Because she isn't angry and she doesn't mind.
CHESTER	H'm?
PATRICIA	About you going off with Mrs Bounty.
CHESTER	But I'm not.
PATRICIA	Even if you are, she isn't angry!
CHESTER	Well, it's nice to know somebody isn't angry.
PATRICIA	It's surprising, too.
CHESTER	Oh?
PATRICIA	Yes.　It must be very hard not to be angry when you've cycled all the way from Littlehampton.
	(CHESTER remains still.　In his tangled web of explanations, Littlehampton rings a bell.)
CHESTER	Littlehampton?

PATRICIA	Yes.
CHESTER	I've heard of that.
PATRICIA	Perhaps there's something there that you want to forget?
CHESTER	(amused) Well, whatever it is, I <u>have</u> forgotten! (Remembering suddenly.) My mother!
PATRICIA	What?
	(He comes down to C.)
CHESTER	It's not my mother, is it?
PATRICIA	Your mother doesn't ride a bicycle.
CHESTER	True.
PATRICIA	She doesn't live in Littlehampton, either.
CHESTER	Doesn't she?
PATRICIA	Stoke Poges.
CHESTER	(delighted) Oh, that's good!
PATRICIA	Why?
CHESTER	I didn't think I knew anybody who lived in Stoke Poges. (Thoughtfully.) I'm sure I told <u>some</u>body she lived in Littlehampton –
PATRICIA	That wouldn't be surprising. You've lied about almost everything else.
CHESTER	That's not fair!
	(She goes to him.)
PATRICIA	(reasonably) Look – this woman upstairs wouldn't be giving permission for you to go off with Mrs Bounty if you weren't going, now would she?
CHESTER	I don't even know who this strange woman is!
PATRICIA	Gladys.
CHESTER	What?
PATRICIA	That's her name – Gladys.
CHESTER	Gladys from Littlehampton?

PATRICIA   Yes.

CHESTER   That rings a bell. She - er - she doesn't play the piano, by any chance, does she?

PATRICIA   Yes.

CHESTER   Oh, my God -

PATRICIA   You do know her!

CHESTER   Well, I don't know her exactly. But I - I've heard about her. And I can tell you one thing - it can't be her!

PATRICIA   Are you sure?

CHESTER   Absolutely positive!   (He moves away below her to D. R.)

PATRICIA   How can you be so certain?

CHESTER   Well - er - because - I - The Gladys I've heard of doesn't ride a bicycle.

PATRICIA   Extraordinary.

CHESTER   Oh, I dunno. I know a lot of people who don't ride bicycles. I had an uncle who tried for years -

PATRICIA   I mean, extraordinary - two Gladyses from Little-hampton who both play the piano!

CHESTER   He kept falling off.

PATRICIA   Who?

CHESTER   My uncle.

PATRICIA   I don't care about your uncle!

CHESTER   He was a very nice man. He just couldn't ride a bicycle.

(She goes to him.)

PATRICIA   Look, if the upstairs Gladys isn't the one you're thinking of, then who is she?

CHESTER   That's what I'd like to know -   But whoever it is, I don't need her permission because I'm not.

PATRICIA   Not?

CHESTER	Going off with Mrs Bounty.
PATRICIA	She said you were.
CHESTER	She misunderstood. That's all. I wouldn't dream of going off with her.
PATRICIA	I wish I could believe you –
CHESTER	Darling – Oh, good.
PATRICIA	What?
CHESTER	You didn't stop me. Darling – look at me. Look into my eyes.
PATRICIA	(resigned) Oh – all right.
	(She comes closer and looks into his eyes.)
CHESTER	Now – do I look like a liar? (A longish pause.) I'll ask you another question –
PATRICIA	I want to believe you.
CHESTER	Then do. (Gently.) Please.
	(A small pause. She melts, smiles and they kiss. ABEL comes in from the kitchen.)
ABEL	You two at it again?
	(They separate.)
	You can't leave it alone, can you, sir?
PATRICIA	(turning) I beg your pardon?
ABEL	Oh, hullo, miss. I didn't know it was you.
PATRICIA	Who did you think it was, then?
CHESTER	Don't take any notice of him. He's never been the same since he got out his primus. What do you want, Abel?
ABEL	It's her ladyship. She needs help.
CHESTER	What's happened to her?
ABEL	It's the corned beef hash, sir.
CHESTER	There are two of you out there. Surely you can manage?

ABEL	Every time I try to help she tells me to go and wash my hands.
PATRICIA	Quite right, too. We don't want the food tasting of paraffin.
ABEL	I dunno. Might be an improvement.
PATRICIA	I'll come and help, Mr Bounty.
ABEL	Thank you, miss. (He goes out to the kitchen.)
PATRICIA	(to CHESTER) You can open the wine.
CHESTER	(his eyes lighting up) Is there some?
PATRICIA	Over there.
CHESTER	Darling, you think of everything!
PATRICIA	With you around I have to.

(CHESTER starts for the wine but sees the vase. He picks it up.)

CHESTER	What's this?
PATRICIA	Ancient pottery. Miss Partridge found it in the cellar.
CHESTER	(alarmed) She didn't go into the cellar?
PATRICIA	Yes.
CHESTER	Oh, my God! (He puts the vase down again.)
PATRICIA	What's the matter?
CHESTER	You'll have to know sooner or later. That place is full of dynamite!
PATRICIA	Now don't you start!
CHESTER	What?
PATRICIA	That's what she said.
CHESTER	Miss Partridge?
MISS P	(looking up) Ah! Have you changed your mind?
CHESTER	What?
MISS P	I've still got that Marmite sandwich.
CHESTER	No, thank you, Miss Partridge. (To PATRICIA.)

	What did she say?
PATRICIA	That she'd found lots of little sticks in boxes.
CHESTER	There you are! Dynamite!
PATRICIA	Don't be silly, darling! How could it be dynamite?
CHESTER	Well, it's not Blackpool rock!
PATRICIA	You surely don't expect me to believe that, do you?
CHESTER	But it's true! They're going to blow this place up tomorrow. That's why I wanted us to leave!
PATRICIA	(getting angry) Honestly, darling! I don't know what's come over you. I realise that all of a sudden you don't want us to live here, but there's no need to make up stories like that to get rid of me! (And she sweeps off into the kitchen.)
	(CHESTER looks defeated and goes to get a bottle of wine out of the carrier bag that PATRICIA has left near the front door. He is preparing to open it happily when CAROL and MRS BOUNTY come downstairs to U.C.)
CAROL	There he is!
CHESTER	What?
CAROL	We've been standing outside the lavatory.
CHESTER	I thought you might have been.
CAROL	And you're down here.
CHESTER	(cheerfully) Opening a bottle of wine.
CAROL	We've been standing there for ages!
CHESTER	There's another one down here. There was no need to queue.
CAROL	You'd locked the door.
CHESTER	I usually do.
CAROL	But how did you get out?
CHESTER	Through the window and down the tree.
CAROL	Anyway, you're here. That's the main thing.

CHESTER	Is it?
CAROL	Gladys has got something to say to you.
CHESTER	Has she? Oh, good. (He crosses to put down the wine on the table and then reacts.) Who?
CAROL	Gladys. (She indicates MRS BOUNTY.)
CHESTER	Ah - yes - of course. Gladys. (An awkward pause.) Have a good journey?
MRS BOUNTY	Er - yes. Thank you.
CHESTER	Oh, good. Good.
CAROL	I'll leave you two together, then.
CHESTER	Why?
CAROL	I'm sure Gladys would rather talk to you on your own.
CHESTER	Would she?
CAROL	Well - of course. I'll go and put our cases in the car. (She goes towards their cases.)
CHESTER	No!
CAROL	What?
CHESTER	You mustn't do that.
CAROL	It'll save time.
CHESTER	I dare say, but I can't let you go carrying cases about. Little thing like you. Good heavens, what would people think?
CAROL	(to MRS BOUNTY) Isn't he sweet? But, of course, you know that, don't you?
CHESTER	Does she?
CAROL	Well, of course. (To MRS BOUNTY.) I bet he doesn't even let you turn your own music. I'll go and wait upstairs, then. Until you're ready. (She starts to go upstairs.)
CHESTER	I say - you're not going to take your clothes off again, are you?
CAROL	Oh, no. (With a smile.) Not yet, anyway. (She goes.)

(CHESTER turns to MRS BOUNTY, embarrassed and smiles nervously.)

CHESTER	You wouldn't like a Marmite sandwich, would you?
MRS BOUNTY	Well –
MISS P	Oh, dear. I'm afraid I've eaten it now.
CHESTER	Ah. Too late. Sorry.
MRS BOUNTY	It's quite all right. I've got some fish at home.
CHESTER	Oh, I see.
MISS P	(fumbling in her bag) There's a little cake, if anybody would like that.
CHESTER	No, thank you, Miss Partridge. She's got her fish and I've got my hash. Hash and wine. Yes. (To MRS BOUNTY.) They tell me you've come a long way.
MRS BOUNTY	Yes. That's what they told me.
CHESTER	Sorry?
MRS BOUNTY	I think there's been a bit of a misunderstanding.
CHESTER	Really?
MRS BOUNTY	I've only come from the village.
CHESTER	Not from Littlehampton?
MRS BOUNTY	I've never even been there.
CHESTER	(pouring a glass of wine) Really? Good heavens. Neither have I. Perhaps we ought to go sometime. Might be rather nice. You never know. Well, well! Oh, dear, oh, dear!
MRS BOUNTY	Don't you know who I am?
CHESTER	Er – well – actually – no. (He takes a drink of wine.)
MRS BOUNTY	I'm Mrs Bounty.
	(CHESTER nearly chokes.)
CHESTER	Mrs Bounty?
MRS BOUNTY	Yes.

CHESTER	You can't be that!
MRS BOUNTY	Why not?
CHESTER	We've got one of those already!
MRS BOUNTY	Eh?
CHESTER	You mean you belong to Abel?
MRS BOUNTY	I'm his wife.
CHESTER	The one who was here today?
MRS BOUNTY	We started upstairs in the bedroom –
CHESTER } MRS BOUNTY)	and carried on all morning!
CHESTER	And you went out and I came in?
MRS BOUNTY	Yes.
CHESTER	And now you're here?
MRS BOUNTY	I'm here for him. He's late.
CHESTER	Well, you'll have to go and wait.
MRS BOUNTY	Wait?
CHESTER	Yes. Get on your bike, go home and wait. I can't have you here. Not any part of you.
	(He urges her towards the door, but she turns back to him.)
MRS BOUNTY	But I've come special.
CHESTER	Special or not, I can't have you seen.
MRS BOUNTY	I've been seen already.
CHESTER	By many?
MRS BOUNTY	By most.
CHESTER	Worse and worse!
MRS BOUNTY	Why can't I be seen?
CHESTER	Well, the thing is –
MISS P	Are you sure you wouldn't like a cake while you're waiting?

CHESTER	Quite sure, thank you. (To MRS BOUNTY.) The thing is I didn't expect you back, and I got into a bit of trouble with this girl –
MRS BOUNTY	Oooh –
CHESTER	Not that sort of trouble. But my wife –
MRS BOUNTY	Is she here?
CHESTER	Yes. And her mother.
MRS BOUNTY	(moving D. R. C.) You are in trouble, aren't you? (He follows her.)
CHESTER	Well, they thought I was going off with this girl, you see.
MRS BOUNTY	The upstairs one?
CHESTER	Yes. And so does she. But I'm not.
MRS BOUNTY	No?
CHESTER	No.
MRS BOUNTY	What's that got to do with me?
CHESTER	Well, the thing is –
MISS P	They're very nice.
CHESTER	(to MISS PARTRIDGE) Yes. I'm sure they are. (To MRS BOUNTY.) The thing is – I said she was Mrs Bounty.
MRS BOUNTY	The upstairs one?
CHESTER	Yes.
MRS BOUNTY	So they think you're going off with me?
CHESTER	Exactly.
MRS BOUNTY	I wish you were!
CHESTER	That's enough of that. So, you see, you can't come here saying you're Mrs Bounty when we've got one already.
MRS BOUNTY	(thoughtfully) Perhaps I could go on being Gladys from Littlehampton?
CHESTER	Ah. Tricky.

MRS BOUNTY   Why?

CHESTER   Because my wife and her mother have never heard of
                Gladys because she doesn't exist, and if she did they
                would have.

MRS BOUNTY   (puzzled)   But the upstairs one - the one who
                thinks you're going off with her but you're not - she's
                heard of Gladys.

CHESTER   Yes. Because I told her. And that's another reason
                you can't be her. Because if you were, you'd give
                your permission for me to go off with the upstairs one
                and that would never do.

                (MRS BOUNTY is now completely bemused.)

MRS BOUNTY   I think the best thing I can do is go home.

CHESTER   Exactly! Is your bike outside?

MRS BOUNTY   Oh, yes.

CHESTER   Good. So you pop out, pop on and pop off. I'll tell
                Abel you've gone to see to the sprouts.

                (A sudden rattle of gunfire - a bit nearer this time.
                They leap into each other's arms. LADY ELROOD
                comes in from the kitchen and sees them.)

LADY E   Chester!

                (They separate in some confusion.)

                Why must you always use gunfire as an excuse for
                proximity?

CHESTER   I didn't know I did that.

LADY E   You even tried it on with me!

CHESTER   (ruefully)   That was a mistake.

LADY E   (to D. C.)   I beg your pardon?

CHESTER   She was frightened. Weren't you? Yes. Very
                frightened. Shaking like a leaf. So I had to protect
                her.

LADY E   Well, at least it makes a change from Mrs Bounty.

CHESTER   Yes, it does, doesn't it?

MISS P	Would you like a cake?
	(LADY ELROOD turns to R. of the sofa.)
LADY	I beg your pardon?
MISS P	Very nice cakes.
LADY E	No, thank you, Miss Partridge. I'm saving myself for the hash.
MISS P	I won't be very long.
LADY E	What?
MISS P	(packing up her picnic) Now sustenance is over I shall return to the cellar.
LADY E	That's quite all right, Miss Partridge. There's no need for you to skulk below stairs.
MISS P	But I can't wait to plunge back into the past.
LADY E	Well, do be careful. Those steps are very steep.
	(LADY ELROOD turns in time to see CHESTER start to take MRS BOUNTY towards the front door.)
	Chester!
	(They stop and turn.)
CHESTER	Yes?
LADY E	Creeping away like a guilty man?
CHESTER	I'm just seeing her off. Waving goodbye. That sort of thing.
LADY E	(moving to them) Seeing her off in spite of gunfire?
CHESTER	Ah - well - you see -
LADY E	If she's shaking like a leaf in here, God knows what she'll be like in the open air. Give her brandy and sit her down.
CHESTER	There isn't any.
LADY E	No brandy? What do you do in an emergency?
CHESTER	I wish I knew!
LADY E	(to MRS BOUNTY) Have I seen you before?
MRS BOUNTY	I'm not sure. (To CHESTER.) Has she?

CHESTER	No.
MRS BOUNTY	(to LADY ELROOD) No.
LADY E	Never?
MRS BOUNTY	(to CHESTER) Never?
CHESTER	Never.
MRS BOUNTY	(to LADY ELROOD) Never.
LADY E	Chester! In that case, perhaps you'd be good enough to introduce us?
CHESTER	I thought you'd say that.
LADY E	Presumably she has a name?
MRS BOUNTY	No!
LADY E	What?
MRS BOUNTY	I live at number twenty-two.
LADY E	You can't go through life with a number! Not even in the country. Come on - introduce us.
CHESTER	Ah - yes. This is Lady Elrood.
LADY E	I know who I am! I want to know who she is!
MRS BOUNTY	So do I -
CHESTER	Well, this is - er - this is my sister!
LADY E	Your sister?!
CHESTER	Yes. She's just arrived on her bicycle.
	(CAROL comes down the stairs, smiling happily, to U.R. of the sofa.)
CAROL	You've had plenty of time. Now can we go?
	(CHESTER freezes. LADY ELROOD glares.)
	There! I told you everything would be all right, didn't I?
	(She begins to sense that all is not plain sailing. PATRICIA comes in from the kitchen.)
PATRICIA	Come on, everybody! Grab a plate. It's ready!
LADY E	Ah, good! And you're just in time!

PATRICIA   Am I?

CHESTER   No!

LADY E   Yes. Come and say hullo to Chester's sister!

                  (PATRICIA and CAROL look astonished.)

PATRICIA)
CAROL   )   (together)   Who?!

                  (Nervously, CHESTER puts a brotherly arm around
                  MRS BOUNTY and smiles. From a kitchen comes
                  a loud cry of pain and a clatter of utensils falling.)

LADY E   What on earth was that?

CHESTER   I bet I know!

LADY E   What?

CHESTER   Mr Bounty's fallen back on his primus!

                  (ABEL comes running out of the kitchen, clutching
                  his behind in agony and moaning in pain. They all
                  react as he runs across below them and out of the
                  front door.)

                  THE CURTAIN FALLS

ACT TWO

Scene Two

Half an hour later.

MRS BOUNTY is shipwrecked on the sofa. She has a
glass of whisky in her hand and is looking dazed.
LORD ELROOD comes on from upstairs, his shotgun
at the ready. He moves quickly to U. R. of the sofa.

ELROOD   I say!

                  (MRS BOUNTY jumps.)

MRS BOUNTY   What's the matter?

ELROOD   There's a man outside sitting in the pond!

MRS BOUNTY   Oh, that'll be Abel cooling off his backside.

ELROOD   In the pond? Doesn't he realise he's a sitting target?

MRS BOUNTY   Don't reckon he's thought about that.

ELROOD   There's not a patch of cover out there, y'know. If
                  the enemy snipers catch sight of him it'll be curtains.

MRS BOUNTY   The way he's feeling now I don't reckon he's bothered
                  about snipers.

ELROOD   I'm not just thinking about <u>him</u>, you know. He'll draw
                  the enemy fire. And that'd mean trouble for all of us.
                  Better get him back into barracks.   (He starts to
                  go back upstairs.)

MRS BOUNTY   What you going to do?

ELROOD   I'll give him a quick blast. That'll soon shift him.
                  (He goes off quickly.)

                  (MRS BOUNTY gets up anxiously, puts down her
                  glass and makes for the stairs.)

MRS BOUNTY   Oh, no! Here – wait a minute! You mustn't do that!
                  Just a minute now!

                  (A loud bang from upstairs.)

                  Oh, no –

                  (She starts for the front door, then goes back to finish

off her whisky first. LORD ELROOD returns,
beaming with joy.)

ELROOD   There! That did the trick all right. Never seen a
              man move so quickly.

              (She goes to the bottom of the stairs.)

MRS BOUNTY   I hope you didn't hit him!

ELROOD   No, no. Just a warning shot across the bows.

              (The front door bursts open and ABEL comes racing
              in. He closes it behind him, breathless and
              bedraggled. He comes down solemnly to C. He is
              carrying a dead rabbit. Quite a pause, then -)

ABEL   Some silly bugger tried to kill me.

              (LORD ELROOD comes to him, delighted.)

ELROOD   Good man! Well done! Nice to see you older men
              can still move, eh? Good example to the youngsters.
              (He pats ABEL on the back.)

ABEL   (wearily)   I might have known it was you. You'd
              better put that thing away before you really hit
              someone.

MRS BOUNTY   (moving to D. L. of ELROOD)   Are you all right?
              Did he miss you?

ABEL   Oh, yes. He missed me all right. Missed me and
              hit that!   (He holds up the dead rabbit.)

ELROOD   Splendid! Capital! The men'll be glad of it.   (He
              takes the rabbit.)

ABEL   (disappointed)   I was thinking I might have it for
              my supper.

ELROOD   No chance of that, I'm afraid. This'll have to be
              shared amongst the men.   (He makes for the
              stairs.)

ABEL   Won't go very far.

ELROOD   Now, remember - in future keep under cover. And if
              you must sit in the pond, for heaven's sake wait until
              it's dark!   (He goes off, carrying the rabbit.)

ABEL   The sooner we get out of here the better. They're all

	barmy, if you ask me.
MRS BOUNTY	You sure you're all right?
ABEL	I dunno. I've never sat on a hot primus stove before. I'm probably marked for life. 'Made in England' for everyone to see.
MRS BOUNTY	I don't know about everyone. Not unless you're going to take your trousers off. You'd better come and sit down.
ABEL	Not sure if I can. Anyhow, I'm soaking wet.
MRS BOUNTY	Then you'll _have_ to take them off, won't you?
ABEL	I've got nothing else to put on. (He sneezes.) I think I've caught my death of cold.
MRS BOUNTY	I'd better get you off home. (She goes to him.)
ABEL	If we try to leave now he'll start shooting again. And I've had enough damage to my backside already.
MRS BOUNTY	Well, you'd better come over by the fire and dry yourself out a bit. Come on, now –
	(She puts her arm around him and starts to help him towards the fire. They get to below the sofa when ABEL has a bad spasm of the shivers and clings, shaking, onto MRS BOUNTY. LADY ELROOD comes in from the kitchen and misunderstands.)
LADY E	(imperiously) Mr Bounty!
	(They separate. The shock of LADY ELROOD's voice stops ABEL's shakes.)
	I'm glad to see you have recovered from your ordeal by fire, but there is no need to run amok!
ABEL	(miserably) I wouldn't know how –
MRS BOUNTY	I was trying to warm him up a bit.
LADY E	You seem to have succeeded. (To ABEL.) If you succumb to this sort of temptation, you have only yourself to blame if your wife runs about loose and takes off her clothes.
ABEL	My wife would never do a thing like that.

LADY E	Poor Mr Bounty! How little you know.
ABEL	(confused) I think I'd better go upstairs and take my trousers off. (He heads for the stairs.)
LADY E	That is no solution!
ABEL	It is for me. I've been sitting in the pond and I'm soaked through. (He goes off upstairs.)
	(LADY ELROOD turns to MRS BOUNTY with a watery smile.)
LADY E	There's still some corned beef hash if you'd like it.
MRS BOUNTY	No fear.
LADY E	What?
MRS BOUNTY	I've had enough, thank you.
LADY E	(with a touch of relish) Well, I'm keeping some for Chester. If ever he re-appears. (Going towards the kitchen.) I think I'll finish off in the kitchen.
MRS BOUNTY	Oh, I can do that –
LADY E	No, no! You stay where you are. You must be tired after your journey. (She goes out to the kitchen.)
	(MRS BOUNTY helps herself to another whisky, thereby finishing the bottle, and sits on the sofa. CAROL comes in from the garden.)
CAROL	I can't find him anywhere!
MRS BOUNTY	He's gone upstairs to take his trousers off.
CAROL	But we're packed and ready to go!
MRS BOUNTY	You and Mr Bounty?
CAROL	(with a smile) No, no! Me and Chester.
MRS BOUNTY	Oh, yes. Well, I don't know where he's got to.
CAROL	Why didn't you say you were his sister?
MRS BOUNTY	I didn't know then.
CAROL	What?
MRS BOUNTY	I mean – I didn't know then what you were talking about.

CAROL   Well, now you're here - perhaps you can help.

MRS BOUNTY   Oh, dear -

                   (CAROL sits beside her.)

CAROL   How do you feel about Gladys?

                   (MRS BOUNTY considers.)

MRS BOUNTY   Gladys?

CAROL   Do you think they should get married?

MRS BOUNTY   Well, I dunno -

CAROL   I mean, your mother and sister have always thought
                   it would be nice for Chester and Gladys to be married
                   but what do you think?

MRS BOUNTY   Not for me to say, is it?

CAROL   Well, you are one of the family. Would you mind
                   very much if they didn't?

MRS BOUNTY   Wouldn't make no difference to me.

CAROL   Oh, good! That's splendid! So perhaps you could
                   speak to Gladys? Next time you're in Littlehampton.
                   If you could explain how we feel then perhaps
                   everything will be all right. After all, she'll have her
                   piano, won't she?

                   (MRS BOUNTY looks bewildered. LADY ELROOD
                   comes in from the kitchen.)

LADY E   Let's hope the gas man arrives bright and early in the
                   morning. Another meal on that primus and I shall
                   feel like a boy scout.

CAROL   (rising, eagerly)   There's good news!

LADY E   (stonily)   I could do with some.

CAROL   You don't have to worry.

LADY E   Indeed?

CAROL   Everything's going to be all right!

LADY E   I'm very glad to hear it.

CAROL   So you needn't worry about Gladys any more!

(LADY ELROOD looks at her for a moment.)

LADY E   Have you gone mad?

(CAROL indicates MRS BOUNTY on the sofa.)

CAROL   (triumphantly)   She's going to do it.

(MRS BOUNTY nods encouragingly.)

LADY E   I must be tired. I seem to have lost track of the conversation.

CAROL   She's going to explain it all to Gladys.

(MRS BOUNTY looks at LADY ELROOD and smiles sweetly.)

MRS BOUNTY   Next time I'm in Littlehampton.

CAROL   So if you see Chester, tell him everything's all right and I'm ready.

(LADY ELROOD remains opaque.)

LADY E   (to MRS BOUNTY)   I see you've finished the whisky.

MRS BOUNTY   Oh - well - there wasn't very much.

LADY E   What a pity. I feel dipsomania hovering above my head.

CAROL   I'm going to look for him in the cellar.

LADY E   What a good idea.

CAROL   It's a funny thing, you know. You're not a bit alike.

LADY E   Who?

CAROL   You two!

LADY E   I can think of no possible reason why we should be.

CAROL   Well, it often happens. I mean, most people say that I'm just like my mother.   (She goes out to the cellar.)

(LADY ELROOD is turned to stone. MRS BOUNTY smiles helpfully, all things to all people.)

LADY E   That girl has taken leave of her senses.

MRS BOUNTY   Well, I do see what she means. I suppose we are related - in a way.

LADY E	(with a withering look) Nothing of the sort. I shall go and unpack. (She goes below the sofa to U.C.)
MRS BOUNTY	(following) I'll come and help you.
LADY E	I can manage perfectly well, thank you very much.
MRS BOUNTY	I mean - if I'm his sister and you're her mother - that must make you practically my mother-in-law.

(LADY ELROOD is in danger of erupting.)

LADY E   You may well be his sister, but that does not make you a relation of mine. I shall go to the bathroom. Perhaps if I take an Alka-Seltzer I can pretend I've had the drinks that went before it.

(She sweeps off upstairs with MRS BOUNTY following her. The moment they have gone, the front door opens slowly and CHESTER comes in cautiously. Satisfied that nobody is about, he closes the door and goes down to get a glass and picks up the whisky bottle. He reacts to the fact that it is empty. PATRICIA appears at the top of the stairs and sees him.)

PATRICIA	So there you are!
CHESTER	(alarmed) What?
PATRICIA	Where have you been hiding?
CHESTER	Hiding? Good heavens, I haven't been hiding.

(She comes down to L. of him.)

PATRICIA	We couldn't find you anywhere.
CHESTER	I was outside.
PATRICIA	We didn't see you.
CHESTER	It was such a lovely evening, I thought what a lovely evening for hiding. I mean - for sitting up here and looking at the sunset.
PATRICIA	Sitting up where?
CHESTER	The tree. Outside. There's a tree outside.
PATRICIA	Never!

CHESTER	Yes. Big sycamore. Outside the little window. You remember? The one I –
PATRICIA	Went down?
CHESTER	Exactly. So it wasn't a strange tree. I'd been there before – you know. Felt quite at home, as a matter of fact, sitting up there amongst the branches.
PATRICIA	I suppose you thought you were safe there?
CHESTER	Yes. I mean – safe and secure. Such a sturdy tree. Been there hundreds of years. Good strong tree.
PATRICIA	So you just sat there looking at the sunset?
CHESTER	Yes. Looking at the sunset and counting.
PATRICIA	Counting?
CHESTER	Curlews. Seem to be a lot of curlews around here. And as I sat in the sturdy sycamore, I thought to myself 'What a lot of curlews. I wonder how many there are'. So I started counting.
PATRICIA	And how many were there?
CHESTER	I dunno. I lost count. (He breaks away D.R.C.)
PATRICIA	You're sure they were curlews you were counting and not sisters?
CHESTER	(turning) Sisters?
PATRICIA	Or perhaps you lost count of them, as well?
CHESTER	Ah. Yes. Sisters. That was a surprise, wasn't it?
PATRICIA	It was rather. Until today I didn't know you had any sisters. Now, all of a sudden, you produce two!
	(CHESTER goes to her quickly.)
CHESTER	Two? Don't tell me somebody else has arrived?
PATRICIA	No, but there was one you stayed with on your way here. Or had you forgotten?
CHESTER	H'm?
PATRICIA	The one whose suitcase you thought you'd taken.
CHESTER	Oh – her!

PATRICIA   Or is this the same one?

CHESTER   No. I don't think so.   (Moves away to below the
                sofa.)

PATRICIA   You don't sound very certain.

CHESTER   I had to think for a minute. I can't be expected to
                remember everything!

                (She moves to R. of him.)

PATRICIA   Not even the number of sisters you've got?

CHESTER   Two. I've always had two.

PATRICIA   Only two? Or can we look forward to any more
                surprises?

CHESTER   Oh, no. Only two.

PATRICIA   She doesn't look very much like you, does she?

CHESTER   Don't you think so?

PATRICIA   Completely different.

CHESTER   Yes. Well, that was my mother's fault.

PATRICIA   I thought it might be.

CHESTER   She would keep giving tea to the postman.

PATRICIA   Well, I'd better go and find somewhere for her to
                sleep, anyway.

CHESTER   She can sleep in the village. She'd rather sleep in
                the village.

PATRICIA   That wouldn't be very kind. After all, she must
                have had quite a journey. Where did she come from,
                by the way?

CHESTER   Ah - er - let me see now. Where was it? She does
                move around rather a lot.

PATRICIA   I see. Well, perhaps she'd better come in with me.

CHESTER   But I shall be there!

PATRICIA   You can sleep on the sofa.   (She starts to go, and
                collects his suitcase on the way.)   And I'll take
                this back upstairs. I'm sure your sister will let you
                change in our room.

(PATRICIA goes off serenely upstairs. CHESTER goes back to the whisky bottle, having forgotten it was empty.)

CHESTER   Oh, blast!

(Desperate, he looks about for a drink. In the manner of 'Days of Wine and Roses', he looks inside a plant pot and finds nothing. Looks in another, finds nothing. Looks in a third, thinks there is nothing and replaces it, moves on, reacts and goes back to it. He looks inside again and finds a small bottle of whisky. He looks delighted, then puzzled, then shrugs it off and gratefully pours a drink and sits on the sofa. As he takes a sip, the door bursts open and the SERGEANT comes in to C.)

SERGEANT   You're still 'ere, then?

CHESTER   Of course I'm still here! Haven't had my dinner yet.

SERGEANT   There's no time for that. On your feet! Let's 'ave you! One-two! One-two! One-two!

(CHESTER rises.)

CHESTER   Don't you ever knock on people's doors?

SERGEANT   I'm a soldier not a travelling salesman.

CHESTER   How did you manage to get here without being shot at? Not like my father-in-law to miss a chance like that.

SERGEANT   I'm not one of your pansy amateurs, you know. I'm a professional. Trained to use the available cover. When I'm down on my knees amongst the trees, you'd never notice me.

CHESTER   Well, I'd try not to.

SERGEANT   Take more than a crazy peer with an itchy trigger finger to stop Her Majesty's forces. You told her, I take it?

CHESTER   Her Majesty?

SERGEANT   Your wife!

CHESTER   Told her?

SERGEANT   About this place - this time tomorrow.

CHESTER	Bang – boom?
SERGEANT	Precisely!
CHESTER	No.
SERGEANT	What?
CHESTER	I didn't.
SERGEANT	You didn't!
CHESTER	No. Well, there's been a lot happening here.
SERGEANT	(moving to D.C.) There'll be a lot more 'appening soon. It'll be no good turning to 'er when you're five 'undred feet up in the air and saying, 'By the way, there's something I wanted to tell you.'
CHESTER	I tried to get her to leave, but she wouldn't. Believe it or not, she actually likes this place.
SERGEANT	You tried to get 'er to go but you didn't tell 'er why?
CHESTER	How could I? I'd feel so silly. Fancy saying to your wife, 'Darling, this is the nice new house I've bought you, and it's going to be blown up tomorrow.' I mean – only an idiot would buy a house like that.
SERGEANT	Exactly!
CHESTER	And you can imagine what her mother would say. She thinks I'm an idiot already. Look, there must be some mistake. It can't be going bang-boom. Not tomorrow.
SERGEANT	Her Majesty's forces don't make mistakes. Not about bang-boom.
	(CHESTER moves away D.L.)
CHESTER	There must be someone I can talk to!
SERGEANT	Have you tried your estate agent?
CHESTER	He's not open till Monday.
SERGEANT	That'll be too late. You'll have gone by then. I should try the vicar.
CHESTER	Vicar?
SERGEANT	Yes. Prayer's about all you've got left.

CHESTER	Look – this exercise of yours – is it so important?
	(The SERGEANT cannot believe his ears. He moves slowly towards CHESTER.)
SERGEANT	Important? Important? It's the defence of the realm. Defence of 'Er Majesty's subjects. You wouldn't want a lot of unseasoned young soldiers running around like a bunch of Girl Guides, would you?
CHESTER	Well, no – but –
SERGEANT	Then they've got to be trained, 'aven't they? Got to be trained somewhere.
CHESTER	But does it have to be my house?
SERGEANT	Oh, dear. Oh, dear me. That's typical, that is. Typical. If it was my 'ouse, that'd be all right, I take it?
CHESTER	Not exactly, no –
SERGEANT	There 'ave got to be sacrifices. If we want our country to be safe and secure, then there 'ave got to be sacrifices.
CHESTER	I'm not asking you to cancel the exercise! But when you get to my house, couldn't you – sort of – go round and leave it where it is?
SERGEANT	You're right in the path of the tanks.
CHESTER	That's not my fault!
SERGEANT	Look, sir – I'll explain.
CHESTER	I wish you would.
	(The SERGEANT gets out a map, sits on the sofa and spreads it out on the coffee table. CHESTER sits beside him to look at the map.)
SERGEANT	Right. Recognise this?
CHESTER	It's a map.
SERGEANT	Oh, you've seen one before? That's a step in the right direction.
CHESTER	I'm not a complete idiot, you know.
SERGEANT	Never mind, sir. None of us are perfect. Now –

	(Indicating with his finger.) over 'ere's the village. Right?
CHESTER	Right.
SERGEANT	Over there – railway station.
CHESTER	Right.
SERGEANT	Down 'ere – hospital.
CHESTER	Nice to know it's handy.
SERGEANT	(with pride) Across 'ere is us – 'Er Majesty's Forces! (Without enthusiasm.) And right up 'ere – you.
	(CHESTER peers at the map.)
CHESTER	That little spot? Good heavens.
SERGEANT	Now – when the exercise begins, H. M. F. push forward 'ere.
CHESTER	H. M. F. ?
SERGEANT	'Er Majesty's Forces.
CHESTER	Yes, of course.
SERGEANT	We push forward Northwards.
CHESTER	Northwards?
SERGEANT	Up 'ere!
CHESTER	Towards me?
SERGEANT	On three fronts.
CHESTER	Three?
SERGEANT	(indicating) 'Ere! 'Ere! And 'ere! We advance. We kill and destroy.
CHESTER	Kill and destroy?
SERGEANT	We shan't be picking daisies, you know.
CHESTER	What a pity.
SERGEANT	Now – the retreating enemy are up 'ere.
CHESTER	Near my house.
SERGEANT	Right. Of course, they're not really there.

CHESTER	The enemy?
SERGEANT	No. We imagine the enemy.
CHESTER	I see.
SERGEANT	As the enemy withdraws –
CHESTER	You mean they aren't even going to put up a fight?
SERGEANT	In the face of 'Er Majesty's Forces they turn pale and run.
CHESTER	Quite right, too.
SERGEANT	But as they go they blow up anything that might be of value to us.
CHESTER	Like my house.
SERGEANT	Exactly.
CHESTER	Look – this is silly of me, I know – but if you're imagining the enemy, couldn't you also imagine my house being blown up?
SERGEANT	These young lads need experience of battle conditions. We can't deprive them of that.
CHESTER	Can't we?
SERGEANT	Seeing this place explode right in front of them is exactly what they need.
CHESTER	Is it?
SERGEANT	So, in a way, you'll be assisting 'Er Majesty.
CHESTER	Will I?
SERGEANT	By 'elping to produce experienced soldiery to defend 'er shores.
CHESTER	(quite pleased) Oh. Well, that's something, I suppose.
	(The SERGEANT folds up the map and puts it away.)
SERGEANT	Right. So that's the good news.
CHESTER	The good news? I wouldn't like to hear the bad.
	(CAROL comes up from the cellar.)
CAROL	Have you heard the good news?

CHESTER	Yes. The sergeant's just been telling me. (He rises and moves D.L.)
	(CAROL comes to D.C.)
CAROL	So there's no need to hang about. We can go.
SERGEANT	She's got the right idea.
CAROL	Thank you. So come on – let's get our cases out to the car –
CHESTER	We can't leave without telling the others.
CAROL	There's no need to. Everything's all right.
CHESTER	Is it?
CAROL	Your sister's going to explain.
CHESTER	Patricia?
CAROL	No – the other one! She's going to go to Littlehampton and talk to Gladys and explain the whole situation. So now there's nothing to stop us.
CHESTER	Oh, dear –
SERGEANT	I'd go if I were you, sir.
CHESTER	I can't! Gladys would never forgive me.
CAROL	She won't mind – really!
CHESTER	What about Patricia and her mother?
CAROL	What?
CHESTER	Er – my mother! I told you how they feel about Gladys.
CAROL	I'll explain it all to them.
CHESTER	No, no! Don't do that!
CAROL	They'll understand.
CHESTER	I doubt it.
CAROL	I'll tell them how we met in the dark at 'The Horse and Groom'. (She goes to her case.)
CHESTER	I wouldn't do that. There's going to be a big enough explosion as it is.
CAROL	What's happened to your case?

CHESTER	What?
CAROL	Suitcase. It was here.
CHESTER	Yes. It's gone.
CAROL	Gone?
CHESTER	Upstairs. It's gone upstairs. It didn't like it down here so it went up there.
CAROL	Who took it?
CHESTER	Oh - er - my sister - Patricia.
CAROL	She is silly.
CHESTER	But she doesn't know.
CAROL	Not about us.
CHESTER	Not about anything! So she's gone to unpack.
CAROL	I'd better go and stop her. (She sets off up the stairs.)
	(CHESTER goes round the sofa to above it.)
CHESTER	No - wait a minute - !
CAROL	Don't be silly, darling. I won't say anything to upset her.
CHESTER	Oh. That's all right, then.
	(CAROL goes.)
SERGEANT	That your wife?
CHESTER	No, it isn't.
SERGEANT	Oh, I see! You 'ave got troubles, 'aven't you?
CHESTER	(crossing to the fireplace) Plenty. So the last thing I want is 'bang-boom' tomorrow night.
SERGEANT	Yes. (He rises.) Well, there's something else.
CHESTER	I thought there might be.
	(The SERGEANT goes to CHESTER.)
SERGEANT	I told you the good news, didn't I?
CHESTER	Yes, you did!

SERGEANT	So now for the bad news.
CHESTER	It can't be worse.
SERGEANT	It's not going to 'appen tomorrow night.
CHESTER	Not?
SERGEANT	No.
CHESTER	That's the bad news?
SERGEANT	Yes.
CHESTER	Sounds more like the good news. No 'bang-boom'?
SERGEANT	No.
CHESTER	Oh, good! But you showed me the map.
SERGEANT	Yes.
CHESTER	Kill and destroy and no picking daisies.
SERGEANT	That's right.
CHESTER	So why isn't it going to happen tomorrow night?
SERGEANT	I'll tell you.
CHESTER	I wish you would.
SERGEANT	Because it's going to 'appen tonight.
CHESTER	Oh, I see. What?!
SERGEANT	Orders from H.Q. The exercise is going to be brought forward twenty-four hours.
CHESTER	Why?
SERGEANT	Got to keep the boys on their toes, 'aven't we? Take 'em by surprise.
CHESTER	Never mind about the boys! What about us?
SERGEANT	Well, that's what I'm 'ere for, isn't it? To warn you.
CHESTER	Thank you very much.
SERGEANT	So don't hang about. Get moving! Let's see your people packed up and out of 'ere in half an hour. Let's 'ave you! On the double! One-two! One-two! One-two!

(A rattle of gunfire.)

CHESTER	Don't say they're starting already! I haven't spoken to the vicar yet.
SERGEANT	Too late for that now. We'll be moving off in ten minutes. (He goes below the sofa to the front door.)
CHESTER	Ten minutes?
SERGEANT	And remember – after tonight, the nation will be in your debt. Don't 'ang about now! One-two! One-two! One-two!

(He goes, on the double, leaving CHESTER a broken man. PATRICIA comes downstairs, grimly carrying her suitcase.)

CHESTER	You've changed your mind, then?
PATRICIA	Yes, I have!
CHESTER	You sound very cross.
PATRICIA	I am cross!
CHESTER	What a pity. I did so want you to be in a good mood.
PATRICIA	It may be all right with Gladys in Littlehampton, but it is not all right with me! (She slams the case down below the front door.)
CHESTER	Somebody's been talking to you, haven't they?

(She turns, angrily.)

PATRICIA	Yes, they have!
CHESTER	I could tell.
PATRICIA	(crossing to R. of the sofa) And I'm not staying in this house a moment longer.
CHESTER	Oh, good.
PATRICIA	What?
CHESTER	I mean – that's what I want.
PATRICIA	I'm sure it is!

(He goes to her.)

CHESTER	I didn't mean that. Look, I can explain –

PATRICIA   I don't know who this Gladys person is, but if you think
            that because she says 'Yes' you can go scorching off
            with Mr Bounty's wife, you've got another think
            coming!

CHESTER   I've got a confession to make.

PATRICIA   I'm sure you have.   (She turns away D. R.)

CHESTER   There isn't any Gladys in Littlehampton.

            (She turns back.)

PATRICIA   There isn't?

CHESTER   Not one that I know. I made her up. Every bit of her.

PATRICIA   Why on earth should you make up a crazy woman who
            plays the piano and rides a bicycle in Littlehampton?

CHESTER   To stop Carol telling you!

PATRICIA   Who the hell's Carol?

CHESTER   Ah. Yes. Mrs Bounty. That's her name - Carol
            Bounty.

            (She goes to him.)

PATRICIA   Telling me what?

CHESTER   I beg your pardon?

PATRICIA   What were you trying to stop her telling me?

CHESTER   That we were going off together.

PATRICIA   You and Mrs Bounty?

CHESTER   Yes. No, that makes it worse.

PATRICIA   (turning away R.)   It certainly does!   (She turns
            back.)   You admit you were going off together,
            then?

CHESTER   No! That's what she thought.

PATRICIA   But not what you thought?

CHESTER   No. I never thought at all. Not about that. I mean -
            going off. Never.

PATRICIA   If it wasn't true, why didn't you tell her?

CHESTER   Because if I did, she'd tell you what happened in

	'The Horse and Groom'.
PATRICIA	She already has.
CHESTER	What?
PATRICIA	Upstairs on the landing.
CHESTER	I never went there!
PATRICIA	No – that's where we were when she told me.
CHESTER	All about the saloon bar?
PATRICIA	Yes.
CHESTER	About it being dark?
PATRICIA	Yes.
CHESTER	It isn't true.
PATRICIA	I bet!
CHESTER	There! I knew you'd never believe it.
PATRICIA	And I'll tell you something else I don't believe. That you and I are brother and sister!
CHESTER	(trying to laugh it off) Well, of course we're not, darling. I know that.
PATRICIA	Are you sure? Because that's what 'Carol' thinks.
CHESTER	Does she? Good lord, I wonder what could have given her that impression?
	(CAROL comes downstairs with his suitcase, ready to leave. She moves down to L. of CHESTER.)
CAROL	It's all right, darling. I've told her everything.
CHESTER	Yes, I know you have! More than everything. And I could do with less.
CAROL	So now we don't have to pretend any more. Here's your suitcase, darling.
CHESTER	Thank you. (He takes it.)
CAROL	I put your pyjamas back in.
CHESTER	Oh. Good.
CAROL	And your toothbrush.

CHESTER	Fine. After-shave?
CAROL	Yes.
CHESTER	Good. (He puts the suitcase down.)
CAROL	So now we can really go and get on with it.
CHESTER	What?
CAROL	Come on - I'm all ready!
CHESTER	Yes. I'm sure you are, but - well, there's been a little bit of a misunderstanding.
PATRICIA	(sending him up) Oh, no. Has there really?
CHESTER	Just a little, yes. About so much.
CAROL	You don't have to worry.
CHESTER	Oh, good. I do hate worrying. Don't I?
CAROL	No. It's going to be all right.
CHESTER	How do you know?
CAROL	Because Gladys is going to be as happy as Larry.
CHESTER	I'm so glad. (To PATRICIA.) Gladys is going to be happy. That's good news, isn't it?
CAROL	Your sisters are going to look after her.
CHESTER	That's very kind of them.
CAROL	Yes. I've told them both all about us. And they've been very helpful. Haven't you, Patricia?
	(PATRICIA moves to D. R. of CHESTER.)
PATRICIA	Whatever makes you think that I'm his sister?
CAROL	(after a glance at CHESTER) Because he said you were.
PATRICIA	Did he?
CHESTER	Did I?
CAROL	Yes.
CHESTER	No! Not exactly - you see -
CAROL	You are his sister, aren't you?
PATRICIA	No.

CAROL	What?
PATRICIA	I'm his wife!
CAROL	Chester!
CHESTER	I think I'll go and have my corned beef hash now.
CAROL	No, you won't!
CHESTER	Ah. Later.
CAROL	Is she your wife?
CHESTER	The one here? (Indicating PATRICIA.)
CAROL	Yes.
CHESTER	Yes.
CAROL	Yes?!
CHESTER	Yes.
CAROL	You never said you were married!
CHESTER	I never said I wasn't.
CAROL	Deliberately!
CHESTER	I beg your pardon?
CAROL	You deceived me - deliberately!
CHESTER	Nothing of the sort. You just jumped to conclusions.
CAROL	You could have stopped me.
CHESTER	It was too late. You'd already taken your dress off.
PATRICIA	What?
CHESTER	And how would that have looked? No dress and me.
CAROL	You mean you never meant what you said in the saloon bar?
CHESTER	'The same again'?
CAROL	You said other things as well as that.
CHESTER	Yes. 'Good evening, landlord. Nice evening. What a lovely pub.'
CAROL	You spoke to me!
CHESTER	Did I?

CAROL   'When I come back we'll always be together.'

CHESTER   Ah - yes.

CAROL   You remember saying that?

CHESTER   Not a lot. But maybe.

CAROL   But you didn't mean it?

CHESTER   I meant her.

CAROL   What?

CHESTER   My wife. This one.

PATRICIA   I assume there is only one. Although nothing would
               surprise me now.

CHESTER   Well, of course there's only one. And I was telling
               her that. That when I came to live here we'd always
               be together.   (To CAROL.)   I tried to explain
               but you wouldn't listen.

               (CAROL moves away slowly to D.L.C.)

CAROL   Oh, I see -   (Cheerfully.)   Well - that's all
               right, then.

               (He is surprised by her casual acceptance.)

CHESTER   What?

CAROL   I said that's all right, then.

               (He moves a little towards CAROL.)

CHESTER   You - er - you mean you don't mind?

CAROL   (generously)   No, darling, of course not.

CHESTER   You understand?

CAROL   Everything!

CHESTER   No hard feelings?

CAROL   None at all!

CHESTER   (smiling)   Still friends?

CAROL   Of course.

CHESTER   Well, that's very nice. Very nice indeed.

               (CAROL is moving towards the stairs. He follows.)

	Where are you going?
CAROL	(grimly) To get the shotgun!
CHESTER	What?
PATRICIA	I'll come and help you.
	(As PATRICIA goes to join CAROL, ABEL comes on from upstairs. He has taken off his trousers and has a towel around his middle.)
ABEL	I can't find any trousers anywhere. (Sees the ladies.) Oh, I beg your pardon!
CHESTER	It's quite all right, Abel. Come on in. They've seen Scotsmen before today.
ABEL	(to CAROL) I got my trousers all wet, see? So I had to take 'em off.
CHESTER	(glad of an escape) I'll come and find you a pair.
	(MRS BOUNTY appears at the top of the stairs.)
MRS BOUNTY	What you doing down there with no trousers on?
ABEL	It was you who told me to take 'em off.
MRS BOUNTY	That was up here, not down there!
PATRICIA	(to CHESTER) Can't you get your sister to leave poor Mr Bounty alone?
CHESTER	What? Oh – yes, of course.
	(ABEL goes towards the fireplace.)
ABEL	I'm decent. Got this towel round me, haven't I? They'd see a lot more of me if I was down on the beach at Frinton.
PATRICIA	(moving to above the sofa) We've got good news for you, Mr Bounty.
ABEL	You found a pair of trousers?
PATRICIA	Better than that.
CHESTER	He can't think of anything better than that at the moment. (Breaks away towards the window seat.)
PATRICIA	You don't have to worry about your wife. It was all a misunderstanding.

ABEL	(to CHESTER) What's she talking about?
CHESTER	I wish I knew.
PATRICIA	Chester isn't going away with your wife after all.
ABEL	(to CHESTER) Crossed your mind, then, did it?
CHESTER	Er - not exactly, no.
ABEL	I'm not surprised.
PATRICIA	Anyway, it's all over now. So -
	(She takes CAROL's hand and leads her to ABEL.)
	come along, Carol. Over here.
CAROL	What?
ABEL	What's this all about?
PATRICIA	Go on - kiss her and say it's all right.
	(ABEL and CAROL face each other blankly. MRS BOUNTY comes down to C. fascinated.)
ABEL	Well, I'm sure it's all right. And I'll kiss her if you like. But she's not my wife.
PATRICIA	What? Are you sure?
ABEL	Couldn't make no mistake about that.
PATRICIA	(to CAROL) You're not married to him?
CAROL	I'm not married to anyone!
	(CHESTER creeps away D.R.)
PATRICIA	Chester!
CHESTER	Yes, dear?
	(She crosses below CAROL towards CHESTER.)
PATRICIA	(sweetly) You didn't make that up as well, did you?
CHESTER	Well - not exactly -
ABEL	She's my wife. (Points to MRS BOUNTY.)
CAROL	No, no. She's his sister.
MRS BOUNTY	No, dear. She's his sister. (Points to PATRICIA.)
PATRICIA	No. I'm his wife.

CAROL	(to MRS BOUNTY) So you're Mrs Bounty?
MRS BOUNTY	Yes. I'm his wife.
ABEL	And I'm Mr Bounty.
PATRICIA	And I'm his wife. (Points to CHESTER.)
CAROL	And I'm Carol.
CHESTER	And I'm the Scarlet Pimpernel!
	(LADY ELROOD comes on from upstairs.)
LADY E	I can't get into the bathroom!
CHESTER	Is it a matter of life and death?
LADY E	The door's still locked on the inside.
CHESTER	So it is. I climbed out of the window, didn't I?
LADY E	Well, now you'd better climb back in again.
ABEL	I'll do it, sir.
CHESTER	You can't go climbing trees like that. It's very chilly out.
LADY E	I heard somebody shouting for trousers.
ABEL	It was me.
LADY E	So I see. Here you are!
	(She throws the pair of trousers she was carrying to ABEL. He catches them, thereby releasing the towel from his middle. It falls to the ground, revealing his purple pants. He gathers the towel and tries to cover himself again. With towel and trousers he goes out of the front door in some confusion. LADY ELROOD comes down to L. of MRS BOUNTY and glares at CHESTER.)
	There's hash for you in the kitchen.
CHESTER	There's hash for me out here, too.
PATRICIA	Why did you call her Mrs Bounty when she wasn't?
CHESTER	That was after she took her dress off. I mean, how would that have looked?
CAROL	You didn't complain.

CHESTER	No. But <u>she</u> would have done.
LADY E	And so would I!
CHESTER	What?
LADY E	I feared the worst and now I know.
CHESTER	If you think this is the worst wait till you hear the rest.
LADY E	I always said you should never marry a man who lives near gunfire.
PATRICIA	Oh, shut up, Mother!
LADY E	What?!
PATRICIA	If she wasn't Mrs Bounty, what was she doing here in the first place?
CHESTER	There you are! That's exactly what I thought you'd say.
	(A loud bang from upstairs.)
CAROL	What was that?
LADY E	Well, it's too late for the postman.
	(LORD ELROOD comes racing on.)
ELROOD	There's a man outside climbing up the side of the house!
LADY E	What?
ELROOD	An intruder trying to get into the bathroom! (He races for the front door.)
MRS BOUNTY	You haven't shot him, have you?
ELROOD	Well, he went down a damn sight quicker than he came up!
	(He opens the front door and ABEL comes in, breathless. He now has trousers on.)
ABEL	He tried to kill me again –
LADY E	Darling, you must stop shooting at Mr Bounty. It really isn't fair.
ELROOD	You mean that was <u>you</u> out there on the wall?

ABEL	Who'd you think it was? Adolf Hitler?
ELROOD	You're supposed to be in charge of the kitchen, not sitting about in ponds and climbing up houses. For God's sake, keep out of the firing line! (He goes out, closing the front door behind him.)
LADY E	There's hash in the kitchen, Mr Bounty. That'll put you back on your feet again.
CHESTER	I should think it'll finish him off for good.
ABEL	Very kind of you, I'm sure, but there's fish at home, which is where I wish I was.
MRS BOUNTY	All the same, you'd better have a hot drink before we go.
	(She leads him towards the kitchen.)
ABEL	He could have killed me.
MRS BOUNTY	Don't you worry now. It might have been worse. At least you had your trousers on.
	(They disappear into the kitchen.)
PATRICIA	You still haven't answered my question!
CHESTER	Haven't I?
CAROL	Nor mine!
	(CHESTER crosses to R. of LADY ELROOD.)
CHESTER	Well, there's no time for that. We've got to go.
PATRICIA	What?
CHESTER	All of us!
CAROL	Where?
CHESTER	Anywhere! Away from here!
LADY E	What are you talking about?
CHESTER	Bang-boom! Any minute now. (To PATRICIA.) I did try to tell you.
	(LORD ELROOD comes in quickly.)
ELROOD	They're on the move!
CHESTER	What?

ELROOD	I thought something was afoot.
CHESTER	Yes, it is and more than that.
LADY E	What's going on out there?
ELROOD	Tanks and infantry! Moving in the distance. (Going upstairs.) I'd better get back to my post. Whatever happens - don't fire until they're within range! (He goes off.)
PATRICIA	(to R. of CHESTER) What do you mean 'bang-boom'?
CHESTER	I tried to get you to leave, but you wouldn't.
PATRICIA	Why on earth should we leave because the Army are having manoeuvres?
CHESTER	Because if we don't we shall all be up there singing 'Over the Rainbow'.
CAROL	(moving to below the sofa) What?
CHESTER	That's what he said.
PATRICIA	Who?
CHESTER	The sergeant. He came to warn us. This place is going up!
CAROL	Bang-boom?
CHESTER	Exactly! It's part of the exercise.
PATRICIA	You mean that really was dynamite?
CHESTER	Of course it was!
LADY E	Don't tell me you've bought an exploding house?
PATRICIA	It's not his fault!
CHESTER	We should be pleased.
LADY E	Pleased?
CHESTER	Because - in a way - we'll be helping Her Majesty.
LADY E	Have you taken leave of your senses?
CHESTER	You wouldn't want a lot of unseasoned soldiers running about like Girl Guides, would you?
LADY E	If my son-in-law buys a house for my daughter to

	live in, I do not expect it to erupt like a Roman Candle!
CHESTER	I knew you'd say that.
CAROL	What time's it going to happen?
CHESTER	About half an hour, he said.
CAROL	Well, come on, then! We'd better get out of here quickly! (She picks up a case and makes for the front door.)
LADY E	(making for the stairs) I shall take my bags to 'The Horse and Groom'.
CHESTER	A very good place.
LADY E	I knew you could never be trusted with house purchase. (She goes off upstairs.)
CAROL	Shall I put these in your car?
CHESTER	Yes! Anywhere!
	(CAROL goes out with various cases.)
	(To PATRICIA.) Quickly, darling – there's no time to be lost. On the double! One-two! One-two! One-two!
	(She runs towards the stairs. There is a rattle of gunfire.)
PATRICIA	(loudly, over the gunfire) It wouldn't be so bad if I didn't love you!
CHESTER	(loudly, also) Darling! That's the nicest thing you've said all day!
	(She smiles and runs off upstairs as MISS PARTRIDGE comes out of the cellar. The gunfire fades. CHESTER collects up cases, packages, etc.)
MISS P	I've been studying the foundations.
CHESTER	It's too late for that!
MISS P	This place must have been here for hundreds of years.
CHESTER	Well, it's not going to be here much longer!
MISS P	They knew how to build in those days. This house will still be standing long after we've all gone.

CHESTER   I wouldn't take a bet on it.

                      (The front door opens abruptly and the SERGEANT
                      comes racing in. He is now wearing a steel hat and
                      has a few twigs of camouflage sticking out of his pack.
                      He is carrying a rifle. He comes to R.C.)

SERGEANT   You're still 'ere, then?

CHESTER   All right! All right! We're just going! It can't be
                      time yet. Half an hour, you said.

MISS P   (to R. of the SERGEANT)   Can't you feel the magic
                      of the Middle Ages?

SERGEANT   What's the matter with 'er?

CHESTER   Don't take any notice. She's always plunging back into
                      the past.

MISS P   Did you know you've twigs growing out of the back of
                      your neck?

SERGEANT   (crossly)   Yes, and you're not supposed to be able to
                      see me!

MISS P   Fascinating!

SERGEANT   The rest of your party in the picture now, then?

CHESTER   Yes, they are! We're just leaving.

SERGEANT   What a pity.

CHESTER   What?

SERGEANT   You remember the good news and the bad news?

CHESTER   Yes.

SERGEANT   Well, now I've got some more news.

CHESTER   I think we've got quite enough to be going on with!

                      (The SERGEANT takes out his map and opens it up.)

SERGEANT   Remember this?

CHESTER   How could I forget?

MISS P   Ah, you've got a map of the area. How splendid!
                      (She hovers, watching them.)

                      (CHESTER moves to L. of the SERGEANT.)

SERGEANT   Yes. Now -   (Indicating on the map as before.) over 'ere - the village.

CHESTER   Yes.

SERGEANT   Over there -

CHESTER   Railway station!

SERGEANT   Down 'ere -

CHESTER   Hospital!

SERGEANT   Across 'ere -

CHESTER   Her Majesty's Forces!

SERGEANT   And right up 'ere -

CHESTER   Me!

SERGEANT   Well done, sir! Now -

(He carefully turns the map the other way up.)

CHESTER   What are you doing?

SERGEANT   Now then - Over 'ere - the village.

CHESTER   Yes.

SERGEANT   Over there - railway station.

CHESTER   Yes -

SERGEANT   Across 'ere?

CHESTER   H. M. F.

SERGEANT   And right down 'ere - you.

CHESTER   Right down there?

SERGEANT   Yes.

CHESTER   Not up there?

SERGEANT   No. So when we push forward Northwards up 'ere -

CHESTER   (pointing) I'll be down here!

SERGEANT   Exactly!

CHESTER   Out of the way?

SERGEANT   Correct!

CHESTER	So - so there'll be no 'bang-boom', after all?
SERGEANT	(a little shamefaced) No, sir.
	(A tiny pause, then -)
CHESTER	Well, you've got a nerve, I must say!
SERGEANT	We all make mistakes, sir.
CHESTER	But if you hadn't turned your map the right way up, in half an hour we'd all have been up there singing 'Over the Rainbow'!
	(PATRICIA and LADY ELROOD come hurrying downstairs. They have coats on and are carrying suitcases.)
PATRICIA	Come on, Mother - hurry up!
LADY E	I'm not a racehorse, you know.
PATRICIA	Well, there isn't much time.
	(CHESTER goes U.S. towards them.)
CHESTER	It's all right. You don't have to hurry.
PATRICIA⎫ LADY E ⎬	(together) What?!
CHESTER	You can go back and unpack.
LADY E	You said we were leaving!
CHESTER	Well, now we're not.
PATRICIA	What about 'bang-boom'?
CHESTER	It was a mistake. There isn't going to be one.
PATRICIA	What about the dynamite?
SERGEANT	I'll send the men to move it.
PATRICIA	(delighted) Oh, darling!
LADY E	(coldly) So the sergeant got it wrong?
SERGEANT	Yes, I did, didn't I?
PATRICIA	And you got it right!
CHESTER	(pleased) Yes, I did, didn't I?
	(A rattle of gunfire. MISS PARTRIDGE looks ecstatic.

(CHESTER and PATRICIA embrace.)

MISS P   There they go again! Echoes of the past!

(ABEL and MRS BOUNTY come out of the kitchen, ready for the off.)

ABEL   We'd like to get off home now.

CHESTER   Yes, of course, Abel. Off you go.

ABEL   We'd feel a bit happier if you'd get that gun away from his lordship.

MRS BOUNTY   Abel doesn't want to get home with buckshot in his backside.

CHESTER   Don't worry. I expect he'll give you plenty of start.

(LORD ELROOD comes on from upstairs. He is rather subdued and is looking disappointed.)

ELROOD   I say - they're going in the opposite direction!

SERGEANT   (to CHESTER)   There you are! What did I tell you?

ELROOD   (seeing the SERGEANT)   Good God! Are you here again?

(LORD ELROOD starts down the stairs towards the SERGEANT, bringing his gun up to the ready.)

SERGEANT   No, no! Please! I'm just going!

CHESTER   Yes, I think you'd better. Come on, sergeant! Let's 'ave you! On the double! One-two! One-two! One-two! One-two!

(The others laugh as LORD ELROOD pursues the protesting SERGEANT round the sofa and out through the front door. PATRICIA turns to CHESTER.)

PATRICIA   Darling, is everything really going to be all right?

CHESTER   Yes, of course it is. Nothing else can possibly happen now.

(They embrace. CAROL comes quickly in from outside, smiling broadly.)

CAROL   Chester -

CHESTER   (surfacing)   Yes?

CAROL	There's a lady outside.
CHESTER	What?
CAROL	Asking for you.
CHESTER	But I'm not expecting anyone!
CAROL	Then it'll be a nice surprise, won't it?
CHESTER	Well, who on earth is it?
CAROL	She says her name's Gladys and she's cycled all the way from Littlehampton!
ALL	What?!

They all look astonished and turn to face CHESTER.
He gives a nervous laugh, looking puzzled and
apprehensive. The others close in around him,
waiting for an explanation as -

THE CURTAIN FALLS

PRODUCTION NOTE

PANIC STATIONS marks the return of some of the characters that have been so popular in my earlier farces, 'Wild Goose Chase' and 'Post Horn Gallop'; namely, CHESTER DREADNOUGHT and his wife PATRICIA, LORD and LADY ELROOD, and MISS PARTRIDGE. The play, however, is a completely separate entity and production obviously does not depend upon having any previous knowledge of these characters. However, so many of you seem to have enjoyed presenting the other plays (I'm glad to say!) that I thought perhaps you would like to meet some of the characters again in a brand new farce. I hope I was right.

PANIC STATIONS is a light-hearted romp in which an unfortunate young man finds himself enmeshed in a tangle of misunderstandings and misfortunes, and as he tries to talk his way out of each situation he only gets himself into deeper water as his explanations misfire. CHESTER DREADNOUGHT is a pleasant, appealing man to whom things happen, and the actor who plays him must believe in the situations completely. We feel sorry for him and like him, and therefore enjoy his desperate attempts to get out of trouble.

Make sure you pace yourself carefully and don't take it all at the gallop. Vary your approach to each different situation. It is so easy to fall into the trap of playing the whole thing in a state of jitters, and the audience will soon tire of that. Give yourself time to think. Even the most outrageously funny line is only funny if it is put forward as a serious suggestion in the context of the play and not as a gag.

LORD ELROOD and MISS PARTRIDGE are both eccentric in their ways, but again must be completely wrapped up in their own special worlds and completely believable. ELROOD is military in bearing, wearing country tweeds and a bristling moustache, and has a mischievous twinkle in the eye. MISS PARTRIDGE is intense and voluble, and is so wrapped up in the past that she is unaware of the extraordinary things going on around her.

LADY ELROOD is well-dressed, well-bred and powerful. She moves about like a ship in full sail, sweeping lesser mortals from her path as she goes and providing CHESTER with a splendid foil. Stern-faced and forthright, she would be more than a match for any but the most fearless son-in-law.

The girls, PATRICIA and CAROL, should be a contrast in appearance. PATRICIA is dark, attractive, vivacious and rather sophisticated; CAROL is blonde, her attractions rather less subtle. But she is a pleasant, good-natured, well-spoken girl. She is not a tarty barmaid or anything like that. Simply a nice, enthusiastic girl who is well-endowed by nature. They are both very easy to look at.

ABEL BOUNTY and his WIFE are locals. They are used to the slower pace of the country and are naturally surprised to find themselves in the centre of some rather strange goings-on. Their long-suffering patience and tolerance can be very rewarding.

Finally, there is SERGEANT EVEREST. He is cockney, a typical Army sergeant; forceful and smart with plenty of attack. His three scenes with CHESTER can be high spots of the evening. But the actor must avoid playing every line like a command, and look for the places to vary the style of attack. For instance, on page 114, when he is appalled at CHESTER's suggestion that the Army exercise might not be important, his pace is slower and his volume lower. He simply cannot believe his ears!

The setting should be attractive and pleasant to look at. Old beams and that sort of thing. At the beginning there is a certain untidiness and the occasional cobweb, all of which is transformed in the interval, but don't overdo it. We don't want old newspapers all over the place! At the opening it is raining outside, so the natural source of light is poor, but brighten it up a little with a couple of lamps. Whatever happens do not have the stage too dimly lit. Farce in the dark isn't easy. As soon as the rain stops (page 10) start fading the sunshine up gradually. As it is Spring it will be daylight throughout.

I have put a few stage directions into the script as a guideline, but that is all they are and obviously you will be able to add to or alter these in the light of your own requirements.

Good luck with your production!

DEREK BENFIELD

PROPERTY PLOT

ACT ONE

2 suitcases (off R. CHESTER)
Bottle of whisky (off L. ABEL)
2 whisky glasses (off L. ABEL)
Suitcase (off R. PATRICIA)
Carrier bag (off R. PATRICIA)
  in it:
    Bottle of wine
    Bottle opener
    Assorted items of food
2 suitcases (off R. LADY ELROOD)
Large handbag (off R. MISS
  PARTRIDGE)
  in it:
    Small mallet
    Thermos flask of beef tea
    Packet of sandwiches
    A few small cakes
Tray (off L. ABEL)
  on it:
    4 mugs of tea
Shotgun (off R. LORD ELROOD)
Weekend case (off L. CAROL)
  in it:
    Nightdress
Address book (off L. PATRICIA)

Towel (off L. ABEL)
Trousers for Abel (off L.
  LADY ELROOD)
Rifle (off R. SERGEANT)

Personal:
  Handkerchief (PATRICIA)
  Plan of area (SERGEANT)
  Handbag (PATRICIA)
  Handbag (LADY ELROOD)

EFFECTS

Rain
Gunfire in distance
Car arriving and stopping
Gun shots
Falling saucepans

ACT TWO

Logs (set by fire)
Old map (off L. MISS
  PARTRIDGE)
Paraffin can (off R. ABEL)
Pottery vase (off R. MISS
  PARTRIDGE)
Sticks of dynamite (off R.
  MISS PARTRIDGE)
Rabbit (off R. ABEL)
Plant pots (set)
  in one:
    Small bottle of whisky